THROUGH THE WONDROUS PETALLED EYES OF GOD

Robert Connolly

ARTHUR H. STOCKWELL LTD
Torrs Park, Ilfracombe, Devon, EX34 8BA
Established 1898
www.ahstockwell.co.uk

British Library Cataloguing-in-Publication Data.
A catalogue record for this book is available
from the British Library.

By the same author:
   Saint Marie Antoinette
   The Armageddon Plague
   Alanna's Snow Dream
   The Crooked Road to Heaven

ISBN 978-0-7223-4857-4
Printed in Great Britain by
Arthur H. Stockwell Ltd
Torrs Park   Ilfracombe
Devon EX34 8BA

CONTENTS

THE EVOLUTION OF MIND
(Aspect of Truth)

I am a creative aspect of evolution,
A probing eye of scientific advance,
Weaving a path thru mental obscurity
in search of solution
That lies beyond the instinctive
complexities of ignorance.

But why? Because I know what
I am, who I am and why I am
And the miraculous, creative
fragmentations of interacting physics
Is the unerring guide and I its obedient lamb
And all is done thru the power of
thought without the aid of manipulating tricks.

"And what have I achieved?" One
might ask, but not believe,
The liberation of the spiritual self
from its prison cell in the instinctive nucleus of the mind.
And thru its guiding light I gratefully receive
Pristine knowledge from beyond
the pale of comprehension and oh,
how I am spiritually dined!

Mysterious, unseen energy manifests
itself in untold, animate and inanimate disguises,
To create the global, pulsating tapestry
of life in infinite variety
And is designed and brought into
existence by the supreme intelligence
of the divine Artist in fascinating shapes and sizes,
Complete with distinctive camouflage
markings in colourful propriety.

But why this enormous investment
in living things?
And yet only one species of life
endowed with the sublime gift of
creative intelligence?
Evolution is the all-seeing eye of
scientific advance and ever nearer
to a transmutational conclusion it brings
The creative spirit of man to greet
in ultimate enlightenment his spiritual essence.

THE WINTER FIELD
(Childhood Memories)

By fireside with faithful friends,
gnawing contentedly on meaty bones,
I sometimes sit and reminisce on
childhood days long gone,
Of the ploughman and his team
in the winter field
And of the upturned sod whereupon.

The raucous rooks loudly gathered
to feast on the worms in the wake
of the advancing plough,
Flying to and fro from field
to hedgerow trees where sated
members momentarily perched
And watched the spectacle from naked bough.

As the ploughman and his team
in dedicated toil
Paced from headland to headland
the length of the green field,
With creaking harness and jangling chains
And the furrowed rows to all
admiring eyes loudly appealed.

I remember too the hare leaping
from its tufted form
As the menacing plough tirelessly advanced,
And speeding away with agile ease
towards the sheltering hedgerow,
Whilst the raucous rooks joyfully
revelled and airily danced.

The blackbird, thrush and others
too foraged along the furrowed rows,
For morsels missed by their larger
cousins in their hurried haste.
And the endearing robin, with fiery
breast, was a flash of warmth in the winter cold.
And happy were my eyes to see
the ploughed patch by its presence graced.

And when the ploughman called a halt for rest
His beloved shires obediently obeyed
And the offering of crushed oats in
their nosebags they gratefully addressed,
Whilst the ploughman puffed on his
clay pipe admiring his artful
endeavour and struggle was for a
timeless moment delayed.

And when day's end was by the
fading light embraced
The weary toilers homeward retreated,
Whilst the rooks in happy voice
and winged flight to their woodland
roost slow-paced
And the tawny owl's hoots the
twilight softly greeted.

ODE AU ROUGE-GORGE DE NOËL

Saluts, joli rouge-gorge, petit ami à plumes,
Avec sa poitrine d'orange enflammé,
Comme un petit chevalier ailé
Dans le jardin d'hiver avec les
flocons de neige arrivé,
Chercher les offres éparpillé sur le perchoir,
A qui tu et ses cousins sont bienvenues.

Les petits enfants tu regardent
avec les yeux enchantés par la fenêtre,
Sautillant ici et la becquetant
les miettes d'alimentaire.
Et sa poitrine d'orange de feu est
une flamme de joie,
Une icone pittoresque de Noël est
un vrai partenaire.

Mais hélas, il n'y à aucune
fête de Noël pour toi, petit
Rouge-gorge,
Seulement une lutte sans fin survivre,
En cherchant pour les graines
perdues dans les champs d'automne,
blé, avoine et orge
Et aussi sur les pechoirs dans
les jardins entouré de neige.

Tu es, petit ami, un survivant courageux,
Passant les nuits froides dans ton
petit abri tout seul.
Et je me demande si tu rêves
de jours heureux,
mais dans l'intervalle je toi
souhaite joyeux Noël et rêves
plaisants, petit ami à plumes.

FIRST CONFESSION

I remember well my first confession
at the innocent age of seven,
When I was suddenly and unexpectedly
confronted by reason
On my journey thru life and
at its end hopefully to heaven,
And the coming-of-age event took
place in the summer season.

As I waited in turn with other
unsuspecting boys
And worriedly wondered about
what I was going to confess,
Innocence seemed to have forsaken
me together with all its joys
And I was alone in a crowd with my distress.

When I finally and nervously
entered the dark confessional,
I knelt down, made the sign of the cross and
after stating, "This is my first
confession, Father," I silently waited.
After a seemingly eternal moment
the priest spoke in the manner of a
religious professional.
"What sins does your soul need to be
purged of, my son, before tomorrow's
first Communion is celebrated?"

That was my problem as I couldn't
think of anything I had done that might
be considered as a sinful act.
And as I was too young and naive I
asked for guidance.
"Anger is a sin, my child, and how
many times have you been guilty of the fact?
And how many times have you been
guilty of not addressing its avoidance?"

Even a saint would be guilty of that,
I thought and . . . "A lot of times," I lied.
"Might that have been a hundred times?"
he suggested and added, "Or perhaps
even a hundred times multiplied by a score?"
I did not disagree and asked myself,
'How many times is that?' But I
remained tongue-tied.
I felt I was then condemned as a
sinner and a liar too if nothing more.

"Disobedience to your parents is a
serious sin in the eyes of God.
Have you ever indulged that obstinate trait?"
"Who hasn't?" I silently asked myself, and confessed,
"Yes, Father," as my sweet innocence was
undone with every remindful prod
And I felt estranged from innocence
and inwardly distressed.

"Envy, jealousy, hate and greed, my
child, are also sins that everyone is
guilty of nourishing.
Can you honestly say that you have
never been moved by their whispering temptations?"
"No, Father, I can't." And after a
momentary pause I said, "There seems
to be a lot of sins that I am unaware
of and they seem to be flourishing."
"The list is endless, my son. They are
as numerous as vibrations."

Then I thought to myself, 'Why bother
making a first confession since it's
only an introduction to a state of endless sin?
Why not simply end one's existence
at the innocent age of seven
And say a fond farewell to life, to kith and kin
And spiritually fly away with the
angels to the kingdom of heaven?'

"*In nomine Patris et Filii et Spiritus
Sancti*, my son, your soul is now
purged of dark stains.
And I impose on you as a penance
one decade of the rosary to be in church recited.
Go now, child, and try to avoid the
temptations of sin and the misery of
its guilty pains.
And when you receive your first
Holy Communion tomorrow it will be
your invitation to be with God united."

On departure I knelt in a pew and
silently and solemnly my penance completed.
And afterwards I sat and pondered
on my first confession.

I was not a happy soul. I was sad
and confused and felt my sweet
innocence had been deleted (experience).
It had not been the enlightening I had
been led to believe, but more like
an introduction to depression.

I had come full of hope and spiritual
expectation and that was besieged by doubt.
I was a seven-year-old child ready
to confess to I knew not what,
without hesitation,
And I had felt compelled to lie
thru an innocent mouth.
And I felt completely abandoned
by the spiritual aura of jubilation.

I waited for my school friends until
they had concluded their ordeals.
And then we all wandered home together
discussing the unknown enormity of sin.
We all wished that we could speak
to God direct and make our innocent appeals.
"And how", I reminded all, "are we ever
going to defeat temptation and a
place in heaven win?"

That night in bed alone, listening
to corncrakes as they kept the night awake,
I reflected on my first confession
and I felt that my innocent soul
had been desecrated.
And I prayed for sleep to come so
that my miserable state of mind I
could temporarily forsake,
With all my hopes and aspirations quite deflated.

ODE TO A LATE-FLOWERING SCARLET POPPY

Greetings, fairest flower in the
sun-kissed bosom of old October,
With impressive scarlet face and
dark, appealing eye, in hopeful wait
For love's wandering mediator on the wing,
To honour your presence and
your treasure pollinate.

But you have spread your blushing
petals out of time and out of place,
Beneath these lofty crowns of painted leaves,
Where the spirit of autumn lingers
in artful mood,
Expressing itself in joyful
shades of colour to create
enchanting, nostalgic scenes as it
silently and invisibly weaves.

And you, late poppy, adrift in
autumn's bountiful fold,
A flowering queen in loudest scarlet dress,
Love's iconic hue, but your life
alas is measured in hours,
When you must face your fast-approaching end,
leaving nothing but your memory to
mentally caress.

And even then as I watched in thoughtful admiration,
A whispering breeze wandered past my presence
And momentarily held the scarlet poppy
in its embrace.
And in its wake the poppy's fiery petals
were shed, love's exquisite essence.

And I was left to ponder on its passing,
A late-flowering jewel that called silently
aloud its scarlet greeting
And impressed upon my memory its
haunting image.
And I felt a spiritual affinity with
its rare autumnal meeting.

MYSTERIOUS MARS

Calling Mars, calling Mars,
you strange, mysterious entity.
You are the red planet of which
so little is known,
Beyond your distant, lifeless reality
Wandering thru space colourfully alone.

You lie in a colder zone of space
With atmosphere uninviting
And with unpredictable dust storms
that scar your harrowed face,
Exposing your desolation to the
space probe alighting.

Your size in comparison with
Earth is inferior
And yet your axial rotation
is the same.
But your solar orbit is
understandably superior
Since you are more distantly
sited in the solar-system frame.

Have you always been restricted,
Mars, to your present orbital route
Or did you once upon a time occupy
a more favourable position,
With water washing over your pulsating
face of youth
And a teeming ecosystem flourishing
in addition?

Have you experienced periods of
creature evolution,
Including an era of dinosaurian domination,
Eons before Earth became their host
to exact solution,
By providing for their prolonged animation?

Mars, have you nourished intelligent
forms of life
Capable of creative invention?
If so, did they attain the highest
plain of thought thru intellectual strife
And did they blindly commit the
ultimate act I dare not mention?

But perhaps instead you suffered
a fatal catastrophic event
That caused your evolutionary
advance to be untimely ended,
When your core suddenly and
violently ruptured and into
unimaginable spasms went,
And Olympus Mons fifteen
miles into Martian sky ascended?

It may have resulted from an
asteroid collision
That shook you to your core,
Causing infernos and volcanic emission
Until depleted was your magma store
And outward from your solar orbit
you retreated,
Forced by impact and eruption,
And your atmosphere was by
consequence deleted
And fatal to biological life was
the holocaust of interruption.

Yes, Mars, you have secrets hidden
in your cratered face –
Secrets that may reveal aspects
of your ancient past.
The question is, would those secrets
prove beneficial to Earth's wayward human race
Or would they reveal the awful
truth that time for both is running out all too fast?

IGNORANCE – THE GREATEST THREAT

If the grass stops growing
the human race is doomed.
And yet that is the devastating
scenario we are blindly rushing to create.
On the back of all-consuming
greed, corporately groomed,
By the original, instinctive
primatial traits that man has
thru millennia nourished and
that now usher him to his
inevitable fate.

Fear, lies and violence, the insidious
alliance and defenders of greed,
And used by its perpetrators
to mentally disguise the face of guilt,
Portraying it as the innocent
innovator of growing need,
Whilst the angelic flowers are
expediently sacrificed by the
polluted breath of wilt.

But the Earth's self-regulating
nucleus, the nerve centre of mind,
Has already begun to intervene
in the mixing of the soup.
And ignorant, arrogant, contemptuous
man, who is to the key aspects of
knowledge and mentally blind,
Will be forced to pay the penalty
for his iniquities and will to abject
humility subserviently stoop.

Human populations all over the world
are growing out of control,
And just as worrying is the ever
increasing breeding of domesticated
animals for human consumption and
posing a serious threat,
Forcing the Earth's self-regulating
system to diversify and keep on
track the futuristic goal,
Or forsake the chosen wayward
species of life and let man's
existence into oblivion set.

$E = MC^2$

Einstein's wondrous equation of relativity
That sparked a revolution in the
infinite field of science,
Unveiling the mystery of particle
physics and exposing simplicity
In the thrall of the guiding light
of evolutionary advance and with its compliance.

As frenzied mental configurations
finally unlocked the door that led to
the awesome truth of atomic power,
That was equalled only by the
fearful realisation of its
devastating potential.
And even Einstein regretted the
revelation in his finest hour,
Petitioning for its non-proliferation
and suppression as essential.

But the genie was out of the bottle
to tantalise the mentality of man,
Where it danced in configurational
patterns of complicated mental
equations searching for solution,
Whilst warfare was spreading itself
across the world in ever widening span,
Threatening to annihilate the established
economic network of both warring
and trading nations in discreet collusion.

Until the perpetrators of heinous,
unbridled greed, the arrogant, elitist-minded
warlords to unavoidable defeat bowed,
When Einstein's equation was finally
and successfully applied to the creation
of an atomic bomb, no less,
That some defiant, non-compliant
warlords dismissed with arrogant contempt aloud
Until the aftermath of atomic devastation
that forced them to willingly and
humiliatingly capitulate without the
imposition of duress.

And sadly, since that inhumane episode
in recent history, greed has been
reinstated and fostered thru the
subsequent decades in the mentality
of evolving man.
It is his nemesis, the weak link, the
unacceptable, corruptive trait embodied
in the animal instinct of the chosen primate,
That can only succeed in prolonging the
hopeful fulfilment of the joy of
eternal life in God's ultimate divine plan,
That will be held in abeyance until the
human mentality collectively with the
innate spiritual self equate.

As the dedicated scientific-minded
members of society continuously struggle
to configurate particle physics in search of solution,
That will ultimately delete the weak
link in man's psyche, rendering him
mentally and uniquely perfect,
And therewith the triumphal conclusion
to Einstein's far-reaching equation, the
unwritten resolution
That will open the door to the transition
of the spiritual self to the eternal
abode and the joy of unrestricted
and unhindered space exploration direct.

THE LOST SOULS

Who or what is God and where is paradise?
The lost souls ask themselves
and each other, longing for enlightenment,
Whilst their mentally blind shepherds
lead them thru a fantasy wilderness,
exclaiming, "Rejoice!"
And flaunt their elitist attitudes
without entitlement.

Paradise is the spiritual haven in
the nucleus of the human mentality,
Wherein resides man's ethereal self
ever occupied with aspects of creativity,
Tentatively constructing, thru
evolutionary advance, the endless
future round the weaving of the
spiritual adaptability
That will ensure the continuous
existence of eternity.

And God, or the Universal Mind of God,
in fragmented compositions
Is everywhere and in everything
invisibly represented,
Thru the particle physics of existence
that indulges the configurational equations
of life species acquisitions
And hence the untold, miraculous variety
of pulsating life forms out of seemingly
nothing invented.

But pity the lost souls who know
not from whence they came,
Nor indeed the final conclusion at which
they are meant to arrive.
Fear is the psychological means used
to bind them to their ignorant shame
And only blind belief, in whispered
breath, is the impoverished link that
keeps their hopes alive.

Access to the light of truth is freely
available to every hungry seeker
And patient dedication to the task is the
key that unlocks every door
Thru which divine knowledge silently
spills from the voice of the unseen speaker,
Inspiring every soul to appease their
hunger from the endless store.

Heaven hovers near and yet, paradoxically,
far away,
As close to God as one can be or
distantly unaware.
The interpretation of spiritually coded
knowledge can be frustrating and
even cause dismay,
But patient dedication will succeed
and rewarding fruit bear.

ODE TO THE SCARLET POPPY

Where the plough the winter fields addresses
And in its wake the upturned
sod in furrowed rows lies,
To await the spiked
harrow's spring caresses,
Before stone-rolled smooth for
the sowing of the grain under watchful eyes.

There you set your blushing
blooms in loud impressive flushes,
Spread afar in undulating scarlet view,
Whilst the notes of joy spill from
hedgerow blackbirds and thrushes
And from other songbirds too in
inspired harmonious queue.

For timeless moments in sun-swept
fields I watched your fiery heads
waltzing to the caress of a gentle breeze.
And sometimes, when accompanied by a
cornflower, cockle and marigold in
colourful delight,
You were the prima donnas for all
admiring eyes to please,
But yours was the iconic face that
set the all-endearing scene alight.

And on punctuated wasteland sites you
proliferated like brightly glowing
embers amassed,
Creating awe-inspiring scenes of
intense scarlet splendour,
Into whose midst I often gently trespassed.
And to your vibrant, ecstatic aura
of sensuous bliss I did my soul surrender.

Whilst surrounded by a dazzling sea of red,
Where butterflies amorously displayed
above in artistic aerial dance
And honeybees busily gathered pollen
grains from every dark-eyed flower bed,
For service rendered in the essential
art of natural romance.

Among ancient rutted ruins too in ivied dress
I saw your scattered presence
here and there in lonesome mood,
Where haunting memories of bygone
days nostalgically impress
And into one's thoughts invitingly intrude.

And often when rambling alone
along a meandering byway,
Your blushing petals and dark
alluring eye accompanied me,
The wanderer's inspiring companion
with ubiquitous dock and bramble in idle stray,
For close bosom friends are we.

And when your scarlet petals are
suddenly shed at their life's end
It is merely the endless beginning
of your existence –
A winter sleep-time in your
divine seed that spring calls to
wakefulness to newly ascend,
For you are, oh wondrous scarlet
poppy, like all your cousins, impregnated
with eternal resistance.

THE EVOLUTION OF MAN'S GOAL

The magnetic goal of mentally evolving
man is the discovery of true reality,
A state of infallibility and
subservient only to the spirit of God,
Existing in an indestructible body
nourished by the particle physics
of time's ideality
And without dependence on naturally
processed food sources that spring
from the Earth's fertile sod.

It will be an era of uncomplicated
space exploration without the
haunting aspects of fear,
To planets and satellites within and
beyond the solar system in nuclear-powered
space rovers guided by the
intelligence of Universal Mind, so near,
Visiting far-distant solar arenas
where some ideally sited planets
spin in orbital steer,
Awaiting the insemination of the seeds
of life wherein the spark that ignites
time's pulsating breath is activated
in the alien sphere.

But when and where will it all end, if ever?
There is no end, only a continuous,
never-ending beginning in a gigantic
carousel of light,
Where solar time systems with their
fiery cauldrons of pulsating energy their
existences self-perpetuate forever.
Across the infinite universe, the beacons
of boundless energy dance in a spectacle of delight.

Whilst their rotating families of
planets in disciplined orbital spin,
To their maternal gravity-powered
generators' unseen apron strings cling
In colourful carousels of
ring-a-ring-o'-roses wherein
One or more might, with a cacophony
of joyful, pulsating life-sounds, sing.

Belief is the higher echelon of
searching thought,
Where inspiration hovers and feeds
the ingredients of enlightening equations,
But all creative dreams are on the back
of struggle to their conclusions brought,
For struggle is the linchpin of
both mind and body in the realisation
of evolutionary revelations.

ODE TO A NIGHTINGALE

Greetings, oh wondrous little
migrant from Africa far away,
And perched up there above me,
out of sight, in the foliated dress
of a mayflower tree,
From where your sublime, angelic
notes of joy spill in cascading play
And momentarily set my very soul
from its physical attachment free.

To soar on spiritual wings of
inspiration where heaven caresses and reveals
Aspects of truth in configurations of simplicity
That only to a deeply dedicated,
searching mentality appeals,
And from which the future is woven
by like-minded scientific souls
in collective complicity.

But you, all-endearing little nightingale,
lacking colourful highlights to
impress admiring eyes,
Are instead endowed with a maestro's
divinely sounding notes that are
uniquely beautiful, beyond compare.
And your resonating song holds the
attention of every listening ear in
awesome surprise
As you pipe your orchestral composition,
and its joyful sublimity with your
grateful audience you freely share.

You are indeed a model of modesty,
unpretentious little feathered friend,
A shy, reclusive joy to hear, but
not on view,
As you hide yourself among the
sheltering leaves of bush or tree and
to your dedicated art you lovingly attend,
Assuring your brooding love of your
undying loyalty that so sweetly echoes
in cascading noteful queue.

Wing to me, oh wondrous serenading
minstrel of day and night.
What secret joy is yours and yet denied
to mortal souls still mentally blind?
Have you bathed in the illuminated
fountain that is the source of divine light?
And if so is your sublimely rich song
heaven's coded equation still waiting to
be defined?

Oh sing, sing, enchanting little nightingale,
and bathe my mentality in your mystical inspiration,
So that I may honour your memory with
words in cascading rhyme,
Flowing like a streamlet's undulating current
of jubilation
That will endure thru the endless
pulsating breath of time.

THE PLIGHT OF THE ROBIN

Festive greetings, friends.
I am the little robin that flits
about the snowbound gardens in
winter's icy embrace.
And my fiery breast is a glowing
icon among the fluttering diversity
That crowds around the food pile
on the garden bird table with
applauding grace,
In our struggle against the haunting
threat of life's adversity.

Whilst angelic snowflakes silently
descend in unhurried feathery dance,
Piling deep all over the sleeping
exhausted land,
Where survival leans heavily
on the vagaries of chance
And where Jack Frost busily weaves
the threads of ice that over the
surface of pond and lake expand.

I have no home nor cosy bed in
which to pass the cold, dark nights,
But I must seek instead a tiny
haven wherever I am at day's end found.
My sleep is shallow and often
disturbed by strange sounds and frights,
But to my status in life's ecosystem
I am by nature bound.

So please remember me and my cousins
thru the cold winter spread
And help us with offerings in our
struggle to survive,
And we will spill our sweet thanks
in notes of joy when spring again
rises from its spiritual bed
And spreads its green mantle over
the awakening Earth, and how happy
I will be to be still alive.

THE YEW TREE

Tree of mystery and legend believed
to be forever young
And found in places round the
world far-flung,
Where you often thrive on sites
ill-considered for survival
And are revered by inspired minds
that ponder on your earthly role
from the unknown time of your
original arrival.

You are an enigmatic entity, yew tree,
both loved and feared by man and
for good reasons.
You offer cooling shade from the
heat of the summer sun and shelter
from winter's icy breath, rain and
blizzard – a true friend for all seasons.

But the living tissue of your pleasing
presence, including your bark, leaves
and scarlet fruits,
Harbours a poison sap to deter
potential browsers, as do likewise
your ever spreading roots.
The shelter from your dark, close-knit
leafy crowns
And from your often hollowed-out
trunks, during history's turbulent ups and downs,
Protected and soothed the displaced, hunted
wanderers thru the ages.
And gratitude to you, old yew tree, often
spilled from the lips of rebels, villains and sages.

And your poisonous defence has been
utilised by man in diluted form,
Against invasive diseases that round
his earthly presence swarm.
Yes, yew tree, you are indeed an
endearing friend that demands respect,
Adept in the complexities of survival, having
lived thru untold millennia, and still a
haven of knowledge, I suspect.

And what a revelation it would be to
learn the secret of your poisonous entity
That is often surrounded by a spreading
family of self-generated clones, each
embodied with your image and your
unchanging identity.

DIVINE FLOWERS

The seeds are many, but the
flowers are few,
And fewer still are the ever
diminishing concerns of the human race
For the beleaguered Earth's
fast-depleting energy resources
in shrinking queue
That threaten to destabilise the
tapestry of existence
and highlight man's fall from grace
As he blindly designs the
annihilation of his kind
And all species of life on the
earthly paradise,
Without having realised the elusive
quest for the big find
That is the escape route to a
continuous spiritual existence
before the arrival of Armageddon,
and the only condition to fulfil
is the asking price.

We must sow the seeds and cultivate
the divine flowers
And breathe the fragrance of knowledge
that silently spills from the petalled
eyes of God,
And climb the mountains that are
the intellect's challenging towers,
Because we are meant to be the means
thru which existence will continue
in the embodiment of the fragmented
blueprint slowly evolving in the
divine pod.

The global suppression of corporate greed,
And in its wake the cascading deletion
of its myriad of tentacles that mentally
manipulate societies,
Is the dire necessity to speedily undo
the threat of extinction from the
strangling weed,
In order to preserve the tapestry
of life that springs from the nucleus
of existence in colourful diversities.
And man must erase from his mentality
his love affair with greed and its diverse powers
If he is to qualify for an eternal
existence beyond his physical entity.
There is a spiritual goal to be attained,
thru the fragmented aspects of physics
that nourish the divine flowers,
And its legacy for intellectual struggle
is a spiritually guided existence thru eternity.

Without the divine flowers there will
be no seeds of survival.
Greed is man's nemesis, the self-cultivated
soul-destroying demon he must suppress.
It generates all aspects of poverty, and the
consequences are untold afflictions thru deprival.
And if man fails to address his innate
weakness he will inevitably succumb
to his own extinction, no less.

THE WILD FLOWER

I am the wild flower of the
fields, the byways, hills
and wasteland places,
Where I spread my petals, spill
my fragrance and my joy,
As I greet the passing wanderers
of diverse faces.

I am found all over the
beautiful Earth,
Living jewels that nourish
all foraging species of life,
But I too am bound by the
rules of existence
And my success is embodied
in strife.

I secrete energy-rich nectar
to reward the bees
for their tireless endeavours
to ensure my continuous spread.
And my pollen grains, love's
fertilising agents, are also the
building blocks of their honeycombs
and cells,
To store the honey that fortifies
their struggle for survival
thru the winter ahead.

My presence activates the genetics
of jubilation
And my song is blissfully sublime,
but silently sung.
My fragrance transcends the pale
of human comprehension
And bathes the soul in its mysterious
essence that remains forever young.

I am the embodiment of love,
A herald of promise fulfilling.
I inspire the music and song that
ripples thru the springtime air
And to the bosom of an ear comes
softly spilling.

I am endowed with knowledge
that belies my humble status,
And my painted petals and fragrant
eyes exude an aura of affinity.
I am the mysterious, symbolic
face of innocence,
The spiritual medium that enables
one, momentarily, to dwell in the
lap of divinity.

My presence is indeed a reason to rejoice,
For I am to all forms of life a source of joy,
And as long as I exist in my myriad
of disguises
The beautiful Earth and its complex
ecosystem will never die.

THE LEGACY OF THE MENTALLY BLIND

I saw no honeybees today to tell me
all was well,
And noticeably fewer butterflies
skipped thru the perfumed air
in exotic dress.
Bumble queens sounded their presence,
but in diminishing queue,
and that too was a warming knell,
As were the absent notes of corncrakes,
cuckoos and other endearing migrants
visiting less and less.
The wild flowers too are under an
ever increasing threat,
With habitats thoughtlessly destroyed
and pollution insidiously spreading.
And the growing silence is reminiscent
of an atmosphere of death,
As community fear takes root and
concerned voices begin to ask, "Where
are we heading?"

Mentally blind, ignorant, arrogant
man builds his highways that will
take him only to his hell,
Among the remnants of his jungle beginning,
And there, by degrees, stripped of
his creative intelligence, he will
in perpetuity dwell,
A failed experiment that, thru his
prolonged inability to suppress his
cultivated greed, denied him the
glorious opportunity of eternal life winning.

ODE TO NOSTALGIA

Oh, to wander free again among
the fields of home,
By winding hedgerows, streams
and endearing trees,
Where often in my youth I
was wont to roam,
With faithful dogs, thru shady
woods and colourful leas.

And along flowery lanes
with brambled edges,
Where nostalgia oozed from
every nook,
And from mossy rivulets whose
presence forever pledges,
Like adventure spilling from
a wondrous book.

Recalling scenes from bygone times,
When man and beast together
in harmony toiled
And hirelings in the fields
composed their witty rhymes,
Whilst the harvest was in heaps
and bundles piled.

Oh, what joy to stray again
with faithful dogs the byways of home,
Among the proliferating flowers of spring,
Whose secreted wealth was stored
in every golden honeycomb,
To sustain the beloved bees that
tirelessly toiled on the buzzing wing.

Or wander carefree with a
meandering stream,
Along flowery banks by hawthorn hedges,
And feel again the excitement
of a boyhood dream
And listen to the songbirds spill
their noteful pledges.

To see again the brown trout
snap a surface fly,
And the grey heron, like a
sentinel, in the shallows silently aware,
Or a kingfisher in a flash of
iridescent plumage jetting by
And to breathe the fragrance of
bluebells wafting in the languid air.

Or to idle beneath a chestnut's
spreading boughs
And hear the cuckoo's call echo
from afar,
Whilst in the fields grazed
contented cows
And, climbing into the azure, sun-swept
sky, wrapped in song, the skylark
was the star.

Oh, to wander free again with
faithful dogs to haunts of old,
Where wild fruits plumped on bush
and bough,
By sheltered headland, on hill
and wold,
Untouched thru the ages by man
and plough.

And there to be when autumn
colours her leafy crowns
With diverse shades of yellow,
orange and red,
And grasses turn to polished
buffs and browns
As the autumn mist comes
haunting with silent tread.

And there to linger unnoticed with
faithful dogs in autumn's lap,
Filled with nostalgic memories
of old.
And there to stay and fill the
empty gap.
And there to dwell content
within the fold.

THE SINGULARITY

An inconceivable speck of energy
at the tapered end of the imagined
black-hole extension
That is said to hold the
gravity-compressed mass of several
stars in a particle infinitely
smaller than the nucleus of an atom.
And the significance of such an
unimaginable event, even in the
scientific field of physics, is
beyond human comprehension,
And therefore in the configurational
mathematics of equations is
impossible to fathom.

Unless one considers existence as
a possible fantasy complexity
of variations on a theme,
And invisible energy, with its
gravity core, the magical, spiritual
ingredient of the Universal Mind,
That projects images into the mix
of particle physics, from whence
issues, thru ageless time, the tangible dream
Of endless queues of untold, pulsating
creatures whose passing existence
is by time defined.

But the singularity is a tentative
step into the unknown abyss of
the human mentality,
And the incomprehensibility of
the tiniest invisible speck of
energy that can weigh millions
of tons compressed from the mass
of several stars
Is beyond the grasp of the human
psyche and its concept of reality,
Like a secret treasure secure
behind invisible, impenetrable bars.

That tempts the imagination to
explore diverse avenues of thought
to seek logical clarification
Of every aspect of advancement in
the gravitational search for the
ultimate truth that is eternity,
Fragmented into an unimaginable
mass of diverse particles of unseen
matter, linked by the interaction
of creative illumination,
And all subservient to and integral
aspects of the Universal Mind in
whose nucleus lies the binding
force of gravity.

ODE TO A SONG THRUSH

I listened to your artistic efforts,
brave song thrush,
As you struggled to entwine your
notes of joy in exquisite song,
From high among the budded
boughs of a forlorn winter tree
in sleeping hush,
Whilst snowflakes fell in aerial
waltz around me as I slow-paced along.

How undeterred you were by
February's icy breath, believing
that you would succeed,
And how encouraging your zeal
to feathered cousins with the growing
urge to sing,
Whilst clustering snowdrops spread
their fragrant, angelic petals below
in flushes of supportive need,
Where a family of tiny wrens
intermittently appeared above and
disappeared beneath a canopy of
spreading brambles in foraging fling.

Your discordant, inspiring notes
raised my spirits too,
As did the sight of angelic snowdrops
in celestial pose
And feathery snowflakes descending in
silent queue,
And an inner spark of joy displaced
my winter woes.

And my deepest praise to you,
speckle-breasted herald of promise,
reminding all
That withering winter was already
in a state of reluctant retreat,
As the snowdrops bathed in the
sound of your noteful call
And I listened and admired all that
I heard and saw in that scenic site
where I happily wandered on
booted feet.

And soon winter will surrender
to inevitable defeat
And spring will call in bleating
voice from surrounding fields, "Awake!"
And your perfectly entwined notes
of joy, endearing song thrush, will
command attention from every
listening ear they greet,
As the petalled eyes of God, in untold
numbers, from their bulging buds will
in a rush of colourful delight break.

I wait in patient anticipation to
hear again your composition of joy
In sweet cascading spill from your
treetop perch wherever I may be,
And at that same moment feel my spirit
rise to a pinnacle on high,
And there to dwell a timeless moment
wrapped in your exquisite song, truly free.

THE FRAGMENTED ROAD TO ETERNITY

Existence, the pulsating breath
of particle physics in integrating collusion;
And life, the manipulative, creative
art of the Universal Mind in variations on a theme
That are in essence recycling agents
of energy's mass and the perfect solution
To that, on course, ever evolving divine dream.

But how does man fit into this
extravagant equation under invisible construction?
And why is he the only species of
life in which creative intelligence has been invested?
Evolution couldn't function without
reason on the back of instruction,
And success depends on the building
blocks of particle physics being, by
the mentality, in correct configurational order digested.

The seeds are many, but the flowers are few,
As the spirit of cultivation struggles
to establish itself in the nucleus of every grain,
From whence the tapestry of evolutionary
art is patiently woven in extending queue
And the creative spirit must in mental
persuasion engage with the basic
instincts of the primeval brain.

Will the great struggle end in success
or failure, an endless beginning or extinction?
Nothing is certain in the physical
construction of bone, flesh and blood
that must to some degree depend on chance.
Only the spiritual self has the
knowledge to lead the lost souls to
eternal distinction,
But only if instinct can be persuaded
to succumb to the celestial fragrance
of spiritual romance.

A SPRING MORNING

As the cockerel sounded morn
And day was newly born
And drooping flowers with
dew-damp heads
Painted yellow, blue, white and red,
Opened wide their petalled eyes
In a miracle of joys,
I heard the dawn chorus of song
That echoed happily along
The woodland fringes of a lake
Where every eye was wide awake
And every inspired feathered friend
Piped its notes from end to end
In a show of true, instinctive art,
Encouraging every beating heart
To meet the challenges of life
Embodied in endless strife
Regardless of the ever present threat
From the frightening face of death.

I paced, with faithful dogs, by
slow degrees along
The dreamy avenue of song
In a most enlightened mood
Where inspiring thoughts intrude,
Whilst breathing the exotic fragrance
of early bluebells,
Wafting unseen from shady dells,
And out along the nearby hills
Scattered drifts of golden daffodils
Came sweeping down to loudly greet,
Each yellow trumpet a joy complete,
Eager to bathe in the rising sun,
From whose warmth all life forms are spun,
And in a sudden splash of light

It crawled above the crest of an eastern
hill and into sight.

In the wake of a nostalgic dawn
We strayed across a pasture lawn
To see the field daisies of the wild
In crowding clusters piled
And thereabout a hare took fright
And skipped away in dancing flight
Across the rising, bleating hills,
Among the dandelions and daffodils,
And disappeared into a hedge
Close to a woodland edge,
Where raucous rooks in patient toil
Built their sturdy nests in the crudest style.
Then from a beechen bough on high
Came rippling to my ears the notes of joy,
As a song thrush with loving care
Draped with song the morning air
And sounds familiar, by degrees,
Intensified as the busy bees
Became actively engaged
And every waiting flower paged
To fulfil a pressing need
And complete the blessing of the seed
That ensures the future of life's diversity
On the Earth's pulsating eco-university.
And therewith I expressed my thanks
to God for His wondrous creation,
And I mentally embraced the all-endearing
new day's celebration.

THE AUSTERE ROAD TO ENLIGHTENMENT

Out of poverty I have sprung –
That circumstantial trap wherein
Untold songs lie in agitated sleep unsung,
Waiting for illumination to erupt
from the spiritual haven within.

I was born in Dublin city in troubled
times, poverty's child,
When pneumonic plague was decimating
little children in merciless execution.
But I somehow survived the onslaught raging wild,
And I was speedily moved south
to the Slieve Bloom mountains of
Laois, far from the plague's
culling persecution.

And there I grew to adulthood
thru austere years,
Spilling the sweat of my teenage
years in toil among fertile fields,
Where the eyes of God serenely smiled
and the notes of joy were sweet
music to my ears.
And oh, what a feast of knowledge
those distant memories still yield!

I studied long and hard, but pressing
family commitments interrupted my evolving pace,
And my bond of love for siblings made of me a slave,
Whose every ounce of energy spilled
in toiling sweat helped to feed every hungry face,
And memories were all that was left for me to save.

In later years I wandered aimlessly
from job to job and sacrificed all
in my prolonged search for the
enigmatic purpose of existence,
And most important of all to discover
the reason why God endowed man
with the miraculous gift of creative
intelligence, His mysterious legacy.
I spilled my mental sweat in exhausting
bouts of deep thought and was committed
to the task regardless of distance.
And after untold configurations of
mental complexities I was duly rewarded
with enlightenment and the impact of its veracity.
And now I know what I am, who I am
and why I am and the reason why I
was endowed with the gift of creative intelligence.
And that knowledge elevated me to a
higher plain of thought beyond compare,
Where the essence of existence is simplicity
And every human being has the ability,
thru their creative mentalities to seek the
liberating truth if they but dare.

THE ULTIMATE REVELATION

Only thru scientific study alone
can man discover the ultimate truth.
There is no other way because God
is the sole scientific source of all
knowledge and therefore science is God.
He created all that exists and in
the mentality of man He embodied
a microcosm of His creative root,
And with that miraculous gift man
was set free to wander the earthly sod.

To indulge his slowly evolving,
complex mentality in his quest for
knowledge beyond his instinctive abilities,
Thru the elementary principles
of mentally fusing configurations
of particle physics to create
fragmented thought,
Resulting in the linking together
of these basic aspects of creative
intelligence thru the manipulation
of his mind's utilities
That he has, over untold millennia
and guided by the innate spiritual
self, intricately wrought.

But yet, alas, there is a fundamental
weakness in the mental character of
the ever evolving primate,
And that is the dilemma that man,
thru scientific thought, must struggle to address
If he is to advance and discover the
secret of eternal existence in the
realm of the divine climate,
And there rejoice in his new-found
pristine status to equate with God no less.

The processing of his instinctive
self was an evolutionary complexity
established by the infinitely supreme
intelligence of God,
Incorporating a complicated network
of survival techniques from the very beginning
That continues in a state of flux
regardless of climate change and
its effect on food sources that
spring from the earthly sod,
For all is designed and implemented
by the divine self-regulating
faculty of the master and champion of winning.

The bone of contention was the
introduction of the spiritual self,
the miraculous source of creative
intelligence into the primate's instinctive complexity,
Where the latter will gradually become
subservient to the influential presence
of the evolutionary spiritual advance
That will eventually succeed in the
flowering of the divine plan thru
relentless scientific dexterity,
And in its wake existence throughout
the universe to promote and enhance.

Chaos exists only in the human mentality
and is as a consequence of the patient
spiritual weaning of the deeply rooted
instinctive self with dominant attitude,
By the later-introduced spiritual self
with creative intelligence, tentatively
trying to influence and impress its
belligerent counterpart
That is motivated by greed and wayward
dominance and hijacks the creative
abilities of the spiritual self to
intimidate others and on their ignorance intrude.
But time is the weaver of life's
evolutionary tapestry and the creative
spirit is its beating heart.

Fusing and linking configurations of
particle physics of thought into
molecular networks of interactive aspects
of creativity,
Stored in the memory bank of the mentality,
the laboratory of thought particles, the
building blocks of evolution,
Inspiring the mentality of man to continue
the struggle to extricate himself from
the ignorance of obscurity
And advance along the route of the
divine mission that will set man free
to wander safely thru space at its conclusion.

THE MYSTERIOUS HARE

The mysterious hare,
sophisticated cousin of the rabbit,
With unrivalled agility
and speed of foot
that can outpace any would-be
predator as a force of habit.

It is a loner at heart, but shares
the grassy plains
with kith and kin,
And in the mating season
the jack forcibly engages
the jill in boxing rituals
the latter's favour to win,
And their upright hind legs
pugilistic dance
Is the jack's strange yet
vigilant form of romance.

The jill gives birth to fully
furred leverets in mid-May
And they are actively mobile from
the start and within days are
from their birth-form gone,
Dispersed among the tall grasses
or crops in a field in survival stray,
And are at intervals attended by
the jill to suckle and whom they are
for several days dependent on.

The hare spends its rest periods
and overnight in a form in a tuft of long grass,
To where it retreats when dusk
steals over the land half blind,
As the hoots of tawny owls thru

the silent air trespass
And the hare settles in its cosy
sheltering haven safely confined.

It is said that a close encounter
with a hare heralds a pleasant surprise,
And the hare is also believed
to be a bosom friend of fairies
that haunt woodland dells,
Where it has been observed
in conversation with little people
in animal disguise,
Frogs, toads, moles and voles
and hares too among spring's
fragrant bluebells.

And I have seen a lone hare
from time to time sat in upright
restful pose in a woodland clearing,
And I wondered if it had been
aware of my presence as it showed no sign of fear.
Perhaps, I thought, it might be a
fairy disguised as a hare and in
full view appearing,
To assure me that it sensed my caring
nature and my endearing thoughts could hear.

The hare is both an enigmatic
and endearing animal friend,
Inoffensive and a joy to watch
when indulging agile play.
It wanders the countryside
alone and mysteriously curious,
but to what end?
Perhaps it meets with the
fairies and visits fairyland
in some secret way.

DONA RAQUEL

From the idyllic Alpine
valleys of Switzerland she came,
To the Mato Grosso jungle in Brazil,
Where native ignorance, poverty
and disease exposed their shame,
Whilst hunger cried from every
mouth pleading for its fill.

She came unaware of their
plight and of her calling,
But soon found herself overpowered
by sympathy and into a state
of compassion fell.
She was the poor's tangible spirit
of hope and deliverance from their
conditions appalling,
And they gathered round their
new-found saviour and affectionately
named her Dona Raquel!

Nurse, midwife, doctor, dentist, all
compounded into one frail dedicated soul,
Who struggled alone without funding
and without help, whilst resolutely
resisting the temptation to flee.
She spent her savings on medical
supplies for the oppressed poor
and married herself to her role,
Making dangerous unpleasant journeys
thru the jungle to deliver the essential
medication to her impoverished flock, free.

And whatever spilled freely from
nature's cauldron of creativity
She put to use in her extensive field
of work and in every aspect of her activity.
She was the native Indians' only
defence against ignorance, poverty
and disease in a region where no
willing doctor was to be found,
But with the help of those she cared for
a makeshift hospital to accommodate
the ill rose from the jungle ground.

She welcomed all without complaint
and attended to their needs like a loving mother.
And sometimes, when requested, she
trudged thru the Amazon jungle
for hours to ease the suffering of another.
She was the epitome of loving care,
fearlessly struggling against man's
greatest enemy, ignorance, in a land
that should be paradise, but for the
oppressed natives was hell.
She was the light that forced the darkness
to retreat and poverty to follow in
its wake. She was the loved, and most
revered, Dona Raquel.

THE DEATH OF A TREE

They came with tractor and trailer,
With chainsaw and shredder,
With ropes and ladders and with cold intent.
They came to fell an innocent tree,
A haven for wildlife,
a comforting presence.
They came on execution bent.

They gathered round the victim,
an eager pack,
Without sympathy or regret,
Their thoughts on destruction set
And with awesome tools equipped,
All ready to indulge their gruesome act,
The coup de grâce and death.

"Oh, spare me, please,"
I could hear the innocent
tree silently plead.
"Do not lop my limbs nor
deprive me of my crown.
I am an enhancing feature of nature,
an inoffensive instrument
of need in leafy gown.
I neither command nor demand,
And I am a source of food,
protection and shelter to a variety
of life's diversity.
Oh, please hear my supplication
and allow me to continue my existence
in the Earth's biological university."

They slung their ropes and set their ladders
and lopped its boughs one by one
And severed its colourful crown,
And logged its limbless trunk
until all but its stump was gone
And scattered in fragmented lament was its leafy gown.

I could feel its sadness and its pain,
But I was powerless to prevent
its needless demise.
I sat forlorn on its remaining stump,
A sorrowful soul with tear-filled eyes,
Reliving the memory of a long-time
friend, the beautiful tree.
And there all alone I silently
endured my state of misery.

FLOWER OF LOVE

She is the jewel of the mountain,
A flower beautiful and rare,
Fragrantly smiling from her earthly bed
And caressed by the unseen hands of care.
She is silken soft and delighting, a precious joy,
To be admired and loved
and held in awe by the captivated eye.
She is a flower of inspiration
Impregnated with heavenly charm;
She is artistically beautiful and fragile
And must be protected from harm.
She is to me a source of joy,
Richly scented, love's temptation,
As I gaze upon her illuminating
Presence with glowing expectation.
She is a morning rose so enchanting to see,
With eyes ever smiling,
And from their mysterious depths
Her spirit is silently toiling
For release from its prison cell,
where it languishes in isolation,
Patiently waiting for its moment of freedom,
And in its wake the jubilation.
She speaks to me symbolically,
Thru spiritual vibes emanating from her soul,
Whilst heaven hovers near, the sentinel of love,
And I can hear the echo of its angelic bells toll.
Is she the true flower whose fragrance I seek,
And among whose petals I can safely dwell?
I will kiss and caress her and spill my affection
And the spirit of love will silently tell.
She is the fairest flower of the mountain,
A rambling rose in search of bliss,
And I am the lonely wanderer seeking fusion,
Hidden in the mystic aura of her fragrant kiss.

ALONE

I am alone
And so have I always been,
Like a dog with a nutritious bone,
Unheard, but seen.
I am a thinker, very deep.
I thrive on mental exploration,
But my greatest discoveries
to myself I keep,
To avoid the rejection of illumination.
Man is merely a means to an end,
A manipulated entity.
He must on an unseen source depend,
And that source is his true identity.
He is endowed with creative power,
But is threatened by fear
And he can in a moment be made to cower,
And his origin was, physically,
and still is a mere primate here.

Yes, I am alone because
I know the truth.
I found the marrow in the bone
By eating the forbidden fruit,
But the fruit is not forbidden by God
As He symbolically encourages its consumption.
It is man in his restrictive
primatial pod
Who audaciously decides for God
with wayward presumption.

I am alone simply because I am free.
I found the missing link and made
the connection,
And now I can truly see,
Because I have experienced resurrection
From the experiment that was a success
And now points the way to the stars,
Where man will venture, no less,
But first he will come face-to-face
with himself on Mars.

THE EYES OF GOD

By sleeping hedgerows,
in fertile fields and wasteland sites,
On rolling hills, by cascading
rivulets and sinuous streams,
rising from the Earth's green sod,
The spring shoots that will bear
the precious flowers of colourful delights,
In crowds and flushes, in posing
clusters and scattered in mixed queues,
the awe-inspiring, loud appealing,
wondrous petalled eyes of God.

I saw them by sheltered woodland
fringes and in quiet dells,
Angelically defying February's
cold, austere embrace,
Their presence heralding the onset
of spring in her green gown
and snow-white jewels,
Calling to wakefulness the
multitudes that would rise from
every place.

And thru breezy March I watched
imposing spring the landscape rearrange
With dancing daffodils,
clustering daisies and fragrant
violets in delightful spread,
Whilst March hares indulged their
agile boxing skills in their ritual
mating game so quaintly strange,
And reclusive kingcups warmly
smiled their greetings from their
swampland bed.

With faithful dogs I strayed thru
April fields among the proliferating
dandelions in loud accumulations,
Beguilers of the tireless, dedicated
honeybees in continuous contented song,
As they carried the fertilising pollen
grains from flower to flower whilst
collecting their rewards –
Tiny droplets of sweet nectar
secreted by the dandelion stigmas
all day long.

And likewise in shady deciduous woods
where haunting bluebells spread
themselves in extravagant masses
And summon the bees with their
enchanting, languidly wafting exotic fragrance
That also lures the inspiration-seeking
nature lover who gently trespasses
And intricately weaves with words
tales of flowery romance.

And among other untold flowers
of diverse names and colours in endless spread,
Thru merry May and exciting June,
rising from their beds on the fertile sod,
They bear the seeds that are the origin
of every form of life's daily bread,
And they are truly too the awe-inspiring,
all-endearing, wondrous eyes of God.

THE LIMPING MUTE CROW

When first I saw you, crow,
you were quietly foraging in a
woodland glade all alone,
In the compacted leaf litter of
several years.
And nearby lay the decaying
remains of a fallen tree beside
a large moss-covered stone,
Where red ants crowded in
seemingly chaotic rush,
foraging too, no doubt for their
sustenance unknown.

I watched you walk with limping
gait, one leg in twisted pose,
And when you raised your head
to instinctively call, only an almost
inaudible click arose,
Denying you, alas, the means to
engage with other crows.
And I felt a great sympathy for
your plight and wished I could
undo your woes.

Fear not, poor orphan crow,
my gentle tread as I pass beneath
these sheltering trees,
To leave my twice-daily offerings
to ensure you will not from hunger die,
Although your precarious survival
fills me with unease
As I wonder what predator might,
by chance, this way pass by.

Too innocently unaware you seem
to be, poor disabled crow,
When foraging on the woodland ground,
And too conspicuous when perched
on a bough too low.
Oh, do pay heed to the echoes of
distant snapping that advanced
warnings sound.

Sinful is the hunter whose eyes
see you only as target play,
But hopefully your muted voice
will deter his investigation
And I will, poor crow, each night
for your safety pray,
To avert your premature mutilation.

You stand alone, a rejected,
forlorn crow
With muted voice and twisted leg
in daily danger,
A lonely outcast of your kind,
unaware of your woe
And compelled to live alone in
isolation, and your only friend
a caring stranger.

And oh, how I fear to speculate on
your future fate.
I search the woodland glade from
end to end each day,
hoping to see you still alive,
But I wonder too, with growing dismay,
How long beyond each day will
you survive?

THE ANSWER

I listened to the intermittent barking
of a lonely fox and the hooting
of a tawny owl,
carried on the wings of air thru
the darkness of a November night,
As I lay in bed awake, pondering
on the vagaries of life and the
consequences of their minuses
and pluses.
The lonely fox, seeking the company
of a vixen with whom to indulge
the compelling, instinctive urge
to mate with its fulfilling delight,
Whilst the owl's nostalgic
communicating hoots my mind
gently caressed
as I searched thru a mental sea
of fragmented thought particles
for aspects of truth plucked
from passing flushes.

And old November, plagued by
the vagaries of weather most foul,
Lightning flashes and rolling
thunder, stormy gales and driving rain,
But it is in a dreamy state of
semi-hibernation
And the barking of the lonely fox
and the hooting of the owl together
with the sounds of stormy weather are
merely dreamlike lullabies and it
has no need to complain.

The fox is, by nature, content with its
existence, and likewise the owl and
old November,
But man was endowed with creative
intelligence and he is captivated
by its ingeniousness.
His divine gift compels him to mentally
think, create and remember,
And with that innovative ability he
can alter life's mundane course
By weaving the thoughtful threads
of change,
To make every aspect of life more interesting
By the simple art of learning to
arrange and rearrange
The complexities of life to simplify
all creation.
And that has to be the ultimate goal
that drives man on and by degrees
solve the mystery and discover
the revelation
That stands in future patient wait
On the other side of an unseen gate.
Dream on, old November – at least
you know what revelation lies
in wait for you.
Spring is not far away.

LOVE'S ASSASSINATION

A dagger pierced my heart last night,
And from its wound my
love is spilling.
I loved the one who caused
my plight,
And she is now my cup with
sorrow filling.
All was in a lingering moment lost,
Last night when my slight
transgression was coldly greeted
And I was into oblivion tossed,
Whilst her love was callously deleted.
But where was her loving,
enduring quality
And where was her compassion
in my hour of need?
Severed was the bond of equality
And heartbreaking was her deed.
I walked thru the darkness of
the lonely night,
Deeply wounded by her sin,
And I knew the source of my
pain and delight
Was the heart I could never win.
She was to me like an unblemished
morning rose
With fragrant petals softly breathing,
As I watched her in angelic pose
Whilst silent thoughts were love knots weaving.
But in a mood of wayward confusion
Her fairest petals were suddenly shed,
And in my heart her piercing thorn
made painful intrusion
And I was compelled, alone, the night to tread.

Now forlorn I walk the lonely byway,
My shattered dreams, like autumn
leaves, in scattered flight,
And I must endure the burden
of sorrow that hangs on every day
And spill my tears in the solitude
of night.
So farewell, my love, my morning rose,
And farewell to all that might
have been.
You briefly bloomed in colourful pose,
But lacked the qualities to be
my queen.

THE QUEEN BEE

I am a queen bee, the matriarch
of the hive,
Wherein I lay the eggs from
which are born my untold
virgin daughters,
The tireless workers in happy
song that help to keep the
summer days alive
As they service the wild flowers
that bathe in the energising sun
in meadows, on bush and tree
and on riverbanks by cascading waters.
But I produce sons too, idle
drones, in numbers far inferior
to their toil-devoted sisters busily occupied.
They gorge themselves on honey,
unrestricted, and sleep the hours
away among the petals of numerous
flowers everywhere found,
But they are strictly a temporary,
tolerated necessity to the hive's
community and to whose
benevolence they are truly tied.
And their hedonistic lifestyle
lasts until I decide to swarm,
and soon thereafter their
existence is by nature in their
own sorrow drowned.
But I cannot dwell on the vagaries
of life and death,
as I am a living egg-laying machine,
Committed to the task of honeybee
generation and by necessity defended.

My sibling daughters service the
wild flowers and take their
reward of pollen and nectar that
build the comb and fill its cells
with honey to offset
The ever present threat of extinction
that would forever still the awe-inspiring
song I sing and with it our existence
forever ended.
I am a queen, not of pleasure, but of
toil, a devotee to survival.
I play my part and sing my song
of love from sunrise to sunset, content
Until my short life is inevitably
terminated by natural deprival.
But my genes will live on in the
community of the hive when my
life is spent.

A PREDICTION

The end of the great journey draws
ever near,
As the multitudes rush towards
its conclusion.
Unaware of the consequences of
their manipulated fear
They eagerly strive to make
the fatal intrusion.

Into the infinite abyss beyond,
Where memories hover in molecular isolation
To nourish the earthly bond
Thru spiritual invitation.

Intangibility is fragmented matter
Wherein the soul of creation dwells unseen,
Administering to its molecules
of life in earthly scatter,
Thru the influential and
thought-inducing perceptibility
of the gene.

But how was life instigated in the beginning?
And what is the reason for its existence?
Mentalities wrestle with theories
of life's initiation without ever winning,
But success is embodied in the unfolding
of simplicity thru scientific, complex persistence.

Whose probing, fragmented knowledge
will reveal the awesome truth.
But alas, will it be too late to save
the human race,
That may have to begin again from
an alien root
On another planet somewhere in
outer space?

For man is destined to be his own
exterminator,
Thru a fundamental flaw in his
instinctive process.
His creative mentality is his
perpetual generator,
Rewarding his endeavours with
extravagant excess.

Until the ultimate invention is
designed and brought into existence,
Thereby fulfilling the divine plan,
When triggered will be the deterioration
of resistance
And with it the gradual phasing-out
of man.

And Earth will be by then
showing signs of exhaustion,
From the wasteful exploitation of
its resources by the human race.
And man will be left without an option,
And he will fade into his primatial
beginnings without trace.

POVERTY

Oh, poverty!
deprived state of manipulated
ignorance, lamenting pauper
of society's wandering byway,
Ever haunted by the spectre
of want
That is activated by those who
cause dismay
As they greedily indulge to excess
from life's benevolent font.

They are the wolves in innocent disguise,
Who contemptuously wallow in
corruption's wealth.
They condescend merely to deceive
and are the weavers of lies,
As they pile the burden of woe
on the poor with their ungodly stealth.

Oh, poverty!
depressed wanderer of the wilderness,
Where hope struggles to survive
And where deprivation is the root
of illness.
And passing contentment is found
only in the bread that keeps one alive.

How well I know you, poverty,
from the very day that I was born,
When you cradled me in your lap
As need hungrily greeted every morn
And was the circumstantial burden
that triggered the manipulated trap.

That imprisoned me in your sorrow,
Searing into my mentality indelible scars
From those humiliating days of
beg, steal or borrow,
And the slowly passing days were
intangible prison bars.

I was in infancy held in the jaws
of death
And you were powerless to intervene
As I struggled with hungry breath,
But I was rescued by my spiritual
guardian, inherent and unseen.

And thru my childhood years
In your haunting shadow I followed,
And sometimes I spilled my
innocent tears
when a piously composed supplication
was by empty silence swallowed.

And then in my agile years of youth,
When hunger often echoed thru my
empty guts,
I began to hear the whispering voice
of truth,
Beyond religious restrictions and
their supporting struts.

Oh, poverty!
harassed mother of millions,
Whose manipulated souls earn their
pittance with their exhausting sweat,
To plump the more the fatted villains
Who impose your ever present threat.

Reaping by insidious guile the
greatest share of the harvest,
To add to the excesses,
Whilst the poor must share
the unfulfilling rest,
As your children parade in
tattered dresses.

But hope, your overburdened counterpart,
Is the comforting whisperer that keeps
alive the embers
From which a spark of inspiration can newly start
To illuminate the darkness that haunts
your members.

Oh, poverty!
what direful sufferings you endure,
Created by the generations of greed,
Who use their wealth and influence
to callously immure
The deprived multitudes in unnecessary need.

And therewith the imposition of
your plight
That cries out to heaven for relief,
As depression spreads its fearful blight,
Imprisoning the sanity in a web of grief.

And ushering mentalities to the edge of doom,
Where death waits in solemn pose,
Ready to dispatch each battered bloom
And still the echoing sorrow that flows.

Thru the heart of every impoverished soul,
Feeding knowledge to be gleaned
And woven, by degrees, to enhance
an evolutionary goal,
As you are slowly from deprivation weaned.

But, poverty, be patient and endure
yet awhile,
Thru the uncertainties ahead,
And you must encourage hope along
every mile
Until greed is stifled in the sharing
of the bread.

ODE TO AUTUMN

Oh, wise and wondrous season
of bountiful maturation,
In whose colourful embrace
I was anonymously born,
Whilst you loudly greeted from
bush and bough in joyful salutation,
Caressed by time's slow pace with
gently wafting odours of fruitfulness
on a sun-kissed September morn.

And in whose bosom I now sit
with faithful friends beneath a
dappled chestnut tree in nostalgic,
mental stray,
Whilst watching happily twittering
swallows jet in agile play above
the rippling surface of a nearby lake,
Instinctively inspired by the impending
hour of their migratory departure
to Africa far away.
And here and there in fields beyond
I see ageing potato haulms whose
unseen tubers beneath the fertile soil
plump their yields, still wide awake.

And thru the long eyes I see
harebell clusters wandering among the rising hills,
As my mental accolades joyously
cascade on you, benevolent autumn,
robed in rich, artistic dress,
Secreted from your unseen, divine
pallet in appealing splashes, streaks and spills,
Whilst your loud and luscious fruits
are to mature perfection coaxed by
the all-endearing sun in warm caress.

And on which numerous life forms
freely feast among your extravagant diversity,
And on which I too am invited to indulge
my appetite's pleasure
In this wondrous Garden of Eden, autumn's
nutritious university,
Where on delightful display and in
endless queue hang the joyful jewels
of life's pulsating treasure.

You are, gentle autumn, my close bosom
friend and I sense the presence of
your spiritual entity
As I mentally trawl thru your physical
reality and bygone nostalgic,
unforgettable scenes,
Whilst bathing contentedly in the
colourful, fragrant sensuousness of
your sublimity,
For you are life's treasure trove
of awesome means.

You are the aged, mature manifestation
of youthful spring,
A divine diva clothed in rich, gaudy,
foliated dress,
With untold clustering, fruitful
jewels that to your tangible limbs
invitingly cling.
And you do, oh, wondrous autumn,
my very soul impress.

SAVE THE BEES

I wandered with faithful dogs
among fields where proliferating
dandelions excelled in loudest joy
Beneath a sun-soaked April sky where
fair-weather clouds paced along in
scattered procession.
And as my soul bathed in a flowery
aura of contentment I was suddenly
aware of something lacking to both
ear and eye –
The absence of bees and their
orchestrated music of toil that
would give the wondrous scene its
vibrant expression.

But man's greed leaves its indelible
scars wherever he treads,
And in their wake the Earth's beautiful
ecosystem must bear the rising cost,
With species of life, both flora and
fauna, en route to extinction wherever
his poison spreads.
And so it will continue unabating
until all the beauty of the Earth
is forever lost.

Or will man, thru some divine intervention,
Cast aside his mental blindness
and suddenly see the light
That will guide him round the pitfalls
of wayward intention
To the fulfilment of the divine
experiment that will be eternal delight?

Save the bees and keep intact their
symbiotic relationship with the wild flowers,
For the flowers are directly and indirectly
the source of all life's nutrition,
And they are also the celestial beauty of
the Earth, the petalled eyes of God, spilling
their fragrance on the passing hours,
Inspiring all aspects of continuously
evolving intuition.

Man's unbridled greed has turned
time into a ticking bomb with the
potential to annihilate all without exception.
And his divisive nature is the
unreliable linchpin that holds
his stability in place.
But could it all suddenly erupt
in wanton warfare on the back of an
insidious act of deception,
When the Earth's ecosystem and
belligerent man would disappear
forever without trace?

Save the bees, the tireless toilers of summer
days in happy song,
Serenading the flowers whilst spreading
their fertilising joy
To every petalled eye that in untold,
colourful diversity and in multitudes throng,
Caressed by the warmth of the sun's
all-endearing, all-embracing fiery eye.

Or surrender to the fatal fascination
of the suicidal potential
That loudly disguises itself to tempt
blind ambition
In the undoing, by degrees, of all that is
sacrosanct to the Earth's unique tapestry
of life and therefore for its stability.
It is high time to cultivate mental
insight and not idly await the unwanted
arrival of perdition.

WINTER MEMORIES

On New Year's Eve fell silently
the snow
On hills and vales and towns,
And the creatures of the wild came
face-to-face with their greatest foe
As it spread its white mantle
over fields and hills and naked crowns.

Oh, pity the sheep on the
ravaged moor,
In bleating retreat to the
valleys below,
Where evergreen woods defiantly endure
The winter's icy breath and
driven snow.

Beneath endearing, sheltering trees
They gathered in woolly fold,
Silently resting, relieved, at ease,
Safe from the winter's biting,
ravenous cold.

The robin with the snowflakes
to my garden came
In search of nutritious fare,
And in its wake came others
of familiar name
For the offered feast to share.

I watched them flit and hop about
With agile determination
As each fed its hungry mouth
In the loudest jubilation.

And I noticed a little wren
watching from nearby brambles
Snap up the falling crumbs of bread
Lost by squabbling starlings
in aerial scrambles,
And oh, how glad I was to know
the tiny cavalier was fed.

I watched the snowflakes
sweep past my window
In feathery dance of coldest joy
As the icy wind sang its
song of woe
Across the grey, depressing sky.

And I thought of New Year's Day
And what lay in wait ahead,
Beyond the snowbound winter
of dismay,
When spring would rise in
colourful glory from its
fertile bed.

Spreading petalled jewels of delight
Wherever its youthful spirit paces,
Whilst migrants call in happy flight
And joyful are the scenes in
untold places.

So sing your melancholy song,
winter, and spread your cold snow,
And still the waters of ponds
and lakes with your icy breath,
For soon you'll be retreating
with your unwanted woe,
As spring gets ready to cast
its net.

THE CORNCRAKE

Crake-crake, crake-crake –
The call that keeps the
springtime nights awake,
As males their presence in
loudest voice make known,
Eager to fulfil their innate quest
Before the meadow's mown.

Crake-crake, crake-crake,
They call from near and far away,
Like noisy sentinels all night awake,
But rarely seen are they.

They crake warnings to rivals
from staked-out patches,
That they patrol with dedicated
endeavour,
Hoping to attract one of the
later-arriving females whose
innate instinct matches,
and therewith the next generation
of corncrakes is assured,
And the threat of extinction
will, hopefully, be never.

The silent, elusive female
makes haste
To form her cosy nest.
She has no precious time to waste –
She must in eggs and young invest.

Before the meadow's felled,
When chicks are in agile mood,
But to their mother's warning held
When danger threatens to intrude.

I listened to the widespread, incessant
craking of the males whilst in bed
at night,
Until sleep bathed me in its balm.
It was an echoing grating sound,
and not one of delight,
That sawed thru the night-time calm –
Crake-crake, crake-crake.

The males their energy in loud
voice flaunt,
Whilst their mated partners are
silently brooding,
And young cocks, with challenging
calls, their elders taunt,
But they are also wise in the art
of not intruding.

And when the mating time has ended
The males fall silent and soon
thereafter for Africa depart,
Whilst the newly hatched chicks are
by their mothers attended
Until they find their wings, when all
their long journey too will start.

But will they return next year,
With habitats being increasingly restricted,
Or are we, soon, no more that ancient
nostalgic call to hear?
And is the corncrake, alas, thru
man's greedy designs, to be from
our midst permanently evicted?

THE ESSENCE OF TIME

Time is the pulsating breath of existence,
And its beating heart is the
fragmented cumulative effect
of every energy-generating fiery sun
In unrelenting struggle with
nuclear fission thru an endless
battle of resistance,
From which the invisible particle
physics of matter are finely spun.

So since time is existence it is
also in essence the fragmented
matter of mysterious mind that
activates all
And possesses the innate ability,
thru the interactive configurations
of particle physics, to manifest
itself in infinite species of life
And embody in them the evolutionary,
instinctive mechanisms to survive,
however large, however small,
In microcosms of the art of
resistance in endless strife.

Energy, the miraculous, mysterious
invisible force that hides itself
away in everything,
From diversifications of tangible
mass to the infinite, intangible,
unseen aspects of matter,
Is the self-regulating overseer of all
its creations, a universal king,
Alert to all the vibratory changes, their
causes and effects emanating from
their sources in spatial scatter?

And the beautiful Earth, our
all-endearing planet, is, by definition,
an offspring and also a self-regulating entity,
Endowed with the capability of
absorbing its energy needs from
the sun thru a unique filtration
system that deflects the harmful
facets of matter back into space.
And it also has the ability to alter
the tapestry of existence when the
need arises, by juggling the
configurations of the particle physics
of infinity.
And that fact begs the question: is
the human race blindly rushing
to its fatal fall from grace?

Time is all and everything, manifesting
itself in an infinite diversity of
animate and inanimate creations,
All inextricably linked to form the
parasitic universal breadbasket
of survival,
Thru an infallible system of
self-generating life forms and natural
recycling variations
That, if unthreatened by man, would
ensure the continuous presence of
awe-inspiring species of life and
their ever evolving revival.

Why, then, did the Universal Mind of
all creation, or simply God, endow man
with the miraculous gift of creative intelligence
Only to witness him primarily utilise
that precious ability to cultivate
and perpetuate ignorance and greed
in all vile and evil manifestations
in both disguised and undisguised
acts of arrogant defiance?
There is an answer to the question, but,
alas, it is entwined in the complexity
of particle physics, and the search
demands patience and diligence
And can only be discovered thru the
configurational deeply probing eye
of science.

Will the answer be found by the
chosen species, man, before the
human race blindly trespasses
beyond the point of no return?
We are, thru mental neglect, prisoners
of our own belligerent ignorance and
insatiable greed.
But if we are to survive to fulfil the
divine experiment we must strive,
collectively, to embrace the scientific truth
and avoid the threat of the big burn,
And look beyond the physical existence
to a new advanced state of manifestation
thru our spiritual seed.

THE HUMAN FOETUS

I am a human foetus of
miraculous invention,
A developing baby under the
spiritual supervision of God.
I am a fused microcosm of
my parents,
Evolving in my mother's
uterine pod.

My sex has already been decided,
By genetic chance or divine intervention,
And my struggle for survival
is in full swing
Since the moment of my conception.

I am a living entity with a
beating heart
That pumps a blood supply
around my tiny frame
To nourish my developing organs,
But as yet I have no name.

I may be a mite, but I am
toiling hard
To be ready for my birth,
When I am from my mother's
womb delivered,
To breathe my first breath of air
on the welcoming Earth.

I cannot see, but I can feel
The joys and fears of my mother.
And in addition I do not know
If I already have a sister or brother.

My life is in my mother's hands
And her circumstances are unknown to me.
I could be sacrificed before birth
for diverse reasons,
And, alas, I have no defence
and I cannot flee.

But then survival is a game of chance,
Whether in the womb or on the Earth,
And I can only instinctively struggle
to be ready on time,
And hope to meet with my parents'
approval at birth.

My mother's uterine cell is my abode
Until my development is complete,
When I hope to arrive in a perfect state
And be a joy to my parents when we meet.

But I might have genetic faults,
Resulting in disabilities,
And my life after birth might
be severely restricted,
Either physically or thru mental incapabilities.

That would indeed be a terrible shock
to my parents,
Their awaited joy imprisoned in sorrow,
But I pray that I will not be a disappointment
On my arrival in that distant tomorrow.

I must struggle to reach my goal,
Regardless of imperfections.
I am a miraculous creation of the
reproductive process,
Whose timetable, alas, makes no
allowances for corrections.

HEARTBREAK

Heartbreak, when my radiant rose
her petals had untimely shed
And in their wake her haunting
fragrance stilled.
I would no more her pulsating
presence impress
And I am with a great emptiness filled.

My jewel of joy had callously departed,
Her discarded petals around my
aching heart in fragments strewn,
As I bathe in my pool of sorrow
Among the remnants of my ruin.

Oh, sweet love, my source of fragrant joy,
Forlorn I wander with memories of you,
To breathe again the sublime
essence of your flower so fair
And gaze at its mystic eye of
darkest hue.

Your memory embodied in my heart
will never die,
And there it will dwell and live
again in moments of nostalgic reminisce,
Like a radiant rose in colourful dress,
And I will breathe anew the fragrance
of its bliss.

Oh, come, sleep – let not this
heartache linger long,
As sorrow overflows my divine cell.
My love is gone. I know not why,
But I can hear the silent echo
of betrayal's knell.

THE BLACKBIRD

The blackbird spills its notes of joy,
Its rich song of love endearing.
It plies its art and knows
not why;
Nor does its brooding mate
within the range of hearing.

It sings its serenade so appealing;
Its notes of joy thru the
woodland sweetly sound,
Whilst its genes around the inner
eggs are stealing,
As promise newly springs from
the fertile ground.

Where bluebells sweep in colourful splendour,
Their exotic fragrance loitering
beneath the trees,
Where I sit and listen to the
blackbird render
Its notes of joy cascading on the
whispering breeze.

Whilst in the hawthorn tree above me
Its love sits silent in patient brood,
She is assured of her joy to be
As she safely listens in contented mood.

Oh, sing, maestro, sing. Spill your
rippling notes of joy,
Echoing to the bosom of my ear,
Where their memory will nostalgically lie
For me, in my solitude, again to hear.

LIGHT

All is obscurity without light,
And permanent darkness is the
abode of death,
When the light has been extinguished
by night
And time has into emptiness set.

Motion plays a key role in existence.
It generates thru devotion,
Which in turn produces light
thru constricted resistance,
Resulting in fiery explosion.

And friction is the catalyst of light,
Magnetising matter and instigating fusion,
But motion is the driving might
And all four are aspects of the
interchangeable collusion.

The wondrous sun, our source
of light,
A giant cauldron of fiery matter,
A beacon that repels the ever pressing night
Whilst distributing its warmth
in radiated scatter.

Motion generates heat and it makes light,
And each is a counterpart of the
other's intrusions
As they dance together in fragmented delight,
Formulating equations that result
in solutions.

The Earth and all its dependent
forms of life are sustained by light,
Manifesting itself in a myriad of disguises,
And man, the intelligent primate,
manipulates its might,
Even utilising the silent language
with which it advises.

The all-endearing sun is the
solar system's source of power,
Radiating light and warmth thru space.
It is the very essence of every hour,
In every form of life, in every
earthly place.

THE GREY HERON

Like a sculptured image it rigidly
stands, a wary sentinel
In the shallow waters of rivers
and streams.
As silent as its shadow, it makes
not a sound decibel,
Patiently aware in watchful wait,
surrounded by water wherein elusive
life teems.

A predator supreme and to sights
and sounds of danger ever alert,
And with vision evolved to the
highest degree of precision,
It strikes its prey at lightning
speed, an instinctively accurate expert,
And all is completed within the
passing of the fleeting moment of decision.

I watched it by overflowing river weir,
Intermittently snapping up
approaching fishes,
Like an impassive sentry with
black-and-white crest and black
epaulettes, distinctly clear,
Highlighting its bluish-grey-feathered
robe as it indulged its instinctive wishes.

Its size, solitary habit and silence
play a key role in its survival
That has endured throughout the
dinosaurian extension.
It haunts the streams, rivers, swamps
and lakes where its presence is an
unannounced arrival,
And standing motionless waiting for
unsuspecting prey to pass within range
is its only pretension.

Although unimpressive in silent pose
and ungainly in rising flight,
It is a colourful, aristocratic loner
that temporarily suspends its self-imposed
isolation during the mating season,
And like the kingfisher, moorhen and
dipper, is an iconic aspect of rivers and
their sinuous feeders by natural right,
And is also an integral part of the
ecosystem in harmonious cohesion.

Its strange behaviour and habit
betray its dinosaurian identity,
Coldly calculating and patiently exact,
With self-survival its sole unwavering priority
And its modern characteristic plumage
cannot disguise the fact.

THE UNSEEN EYE

The unseen eye sees all,
And all is held in its thrall.
It is the very essence of existence
Unhindered by distance.
The fundamental principle of
existence is motion,
And that too fuels the ingredients
of notion,
From which creative thought springs
And is expressed in all tangible things
That are the products of invention,
Spilling from the mentalities of men
and too numerous to mention.

There is nothing beyond the vision
of the unseen,
Whether in the bowels of the Earth
or on a mountain high.
It regulates the flexible rules
of existence,
Using positive and negative resistance
To ensure the balance of life is kept
in harmonious agreement
And time heals the weeping scars
of bereavement.

Space is an endless sea of intangible
matter ever pulsating,
And time is the infinity of its recycling
existence unabating.
It is the soul of seemingly nothing
Wherein creation steals silently plotting
And the unseen eye is the nucleus of sensitivity,
Without the limited restrictions of
biological visibility.

It is aware of all life's needs
And every pulsating entity from
its benevolence feeds,
Including man, the paradox of creation,
A unique source of invention, but also,
alas, of violation,
And who is now haunted by the
fear of his own extinction
Because of greed, his fatal addiction.
But the unseen eye is aware of
his affliction
And I wonder how long it will be
before his inevitable eviction.

THE HUMAN ENIGMA

We live on a planet that exists
in an infinite spatial expanse,
Spinning on its axis whilst orbiting
the sun in timeless motion.
It is cocooned in an atmosphere of
oxygenated air in unseen molecular dance,
With a myriad of dependants and
seemingly without emotion.

But why? What is the purpose
of existence?
Was it an accidental event or a
deliberate creation?
Why is there disciplined order,
acceptance and resistance?
And what is man's final destination?

Is the Earth a pulsating galaxial station,
Created by space travellers with
intelligence supreme?
Is it one of their experimental life
laboratories of diversification
Or is that just a pipe dream?

Who knows what's happening beyond
the scope of our understanding?
We are mere mortals sculptured from
the minerals of the Earth,
But we will be in the near future
on other planets landing?
And that fact was already known
before man's birth.

The human race is the only form
of life with limitless creative ability,
And we are the evolving precision
tools of a greater, unseen force.
We are also endowed with manipulative
physical powers of agility,
And we were programmed from the
beginning to follow a definite course.

A course that extends beyond our
earthly abode,
Out into the endless extension of
universal space,
Along a timeless invisible road,
Encapsulated in an energised space-
ship in exploratory chase.
And the purpose of our journey
will be, in part, the survival of
the human race,
That is destined to become the victim
of its own insatiable greed,
And we will search for a safe
haven in space,
To fulfil a continuous, endless need.
But what is the compelling force
that drives us to our hell?
It is the divisive war within that
haunts our mentality,
Imprisoning the spiritual self in a
fear-fortified mental cell,
Where it languishes whilst the host
struggles with his sanity.
And the cause of the effect was the fusing
of intelligence and instinct –
An event that is embodied in the
missing link.

The two qualities, both necessities in
intelligent man, were once upon a time distinct,
And the fusing resulted in the primate's
ability to think.

Embodied herein is a clue to
discovering the naked truth
That hovers near, but out of sight.
The spiritual self is not only
the essence of youth,
But also the scientific presence
and guiding light.

SO NEAR AND YET SO FAR AWAY

So near and yet so far away –
The simple truth of an old adage,
So often idly quoted by the lips of dismay,
As mentalities in wayward fantasies engage,
Imagining the opportunities that would arise
If chance had slightly leaned
in their direction,
Opening the door to a multitude of joys,
Believing that wealth is the recipe
for perfection.
But is it not undeniably true
That the best things in life are free
And are ever on unrestricted view
Without the payment of a fee?
And yet the idle fantasies of pleasure,
That for some become tangible realities,
Appealing to those lovers of
wasteful leisure,
Who never seem able to satisfy
their wayward vanities,
That crave endless admiration
And are always dissatisfied with
their generous slice.
They wallow in selfish jubilation
And stand in queue to pay the asking price.

"The grass is greener on the other side," they say,
But logic intervenes and denies.
So near and yet so far away –
One can almost hear the anguished cries
Of those who seek the elusive lady, Chance,
In moments of high expectation,
When fantasies with reality romance
Round the hopes of high remuneration.

But chickens shouldn't be counted
before they are hatched,
As every child is undoubtedly taught
And paupers with their trousers patched
Rue the day their fortunes thru
idle speculation sought.
And yet the greedy trait is ever present
In selfish souls throughout life,
From majestic king to lowly peasant
Whose weakness is interwoven in his strife.
Self-discipline is the art admired
Wherever it may be found,
And always by its counterpart respect inspired
And together in harmonious partnership bound.

So near and yet so far away –
The bridge of truth that spans
the dark abyss.
Unseen by the multitudes of mentally blind that stray
From the narrow path of bliss,
Aimlessly wandering like lost sheep.
At the mercy of circumstantial strife,
They often in their misery weep
And dream of wasteful ways to put
excitement into life,
Indulging in expensive wayward pleasures
That erode the morals of the mind,
Where the seeds of unknown treasures
Lie in dormant sleep behind
The false facades of fantasies in idle flight,
Weaving patterns of gaudy unreality
And by degrees losing sight
Of that inherent quality, sanity,
As they slide into an obscure existence,
Where life is lived in shades of grey,
Just beyond the pale of mental resistance –
So near and yet so far away.

THE EXPERIMENT

Outer space, hauntingly mysterious,
A seemingly vast emptiness,
Except for a tiny collection of
planets and their satellites,
Sparsely scattered across the
spatial expanse of the solar system.
And light years beyond it untold
stars pose in zodiacal patterns
in the endless universe,
Silently exclaiming existence!

From the birth of a star came
the molten mass from which
the Earth evolved,
And in the wake of its fiery birth
it instinctively revolved and
gradually cooled
And with supreme energetic force
Created the infrastructure for life's
fundamental beginnings and set
its course,
Shrouded in complex mystery,
And began its evolutionary advance
Thru the oceans of teeming planktonic
life and beyond,
By divine guidance and not by chance,
Thru the dinosaurian extension
and into the mammalian age and
the emergence of *Homo sapiens*,
The species of life endowed with
creative intelligence, no less,
And in whom so much is invested,
But why, and will the experiment be a success?

THE VIRUS

Unseen, it hovers round the body seeking entry,
And with ill intent cautiously advances,
Noting every aspect of the body's defences,
From which it gleans knowledge
and its strategy enhances
Until its devious plan of
penetration is designed,
When the virus insidiously enters,
spreading its disease,
And the victim is by slow or
fast degrees maligned,
Whilst the body's deceived defences
rally ill at ease,
To confront the fever-generating threat,
And war within the pulsating entity rages,
With every microscopic warrior
fighting for survival
As each invader and defender in
a life-and-death struggle engages.
But nothing beyond the oozing sweat of strife
On the outer flesh is seen
As the fevered body pales
And the face takes on a faint shade of green.
And the tortured mentality in delirious wanderings raves,
With demonic hallucinations
rampaging in fearful waves,
Whilst the proliferating virus, in suicidal mood,
Blindly struggles to achieve an empty success,
Perishing where it dared intrude,
And likewise the body's dedicated
defenders must struggle to impress,
As the battle must be won or lost,
And in that moment of victory or defeat
only the body can be triumphant
or both must pay the fatal cost.

THE MISSING LINK

I found the missing link,
Hidden within the memory
molecules of the mind,
Where the genetic formula
that induced the evolving primate
to think
Lies in fragmented disarray,
waiting to be discovered by those
who can see and yet are blind.

The jungle, the origin of our
beginning, is never far away.
It haunts the outer fringes of sanity,
A dark existence into which one
must not stray
And wherein fear indulges
in profanity.

I am an explorer of deep thought,
Ever searching for avenues
of enlightenment,
Where measures of success are
with dedication bought
And the results are aspects
of excitement.

The Universal Mind exists
in fragmented scatter,
With a microcosm of its nucleus in
every atom,
So that all thought emanates from
unseen, impregnated matter,
But infinite intelligence is beyond
one's ability to fathom.

The missing link was the fusing of
particles of matter
That prepared the primate to play
the role of man
By utilising the process of
evolutionary mutation to flatter
And therewith fulfil the
ingenious plan.

That has infinite potential
In the exploration of the solar
system and beyond,
Which will be in a future age essential,
When the Earth's energy sources
are depleted and it becomes an
empty pond.

By then man will have completed
his experimental role
And he will be relieved of his burden
of responsibility,
Whilst the essence of his spiritual soul
Will continue experimenting
with probability.

MY LADY FAIR

When first I saw my lady fair
'Twas in shadow-haunting candlelight,
And all about her golden hair
Jewelled roses bloomed bright.
Her eyes shone with a mystic glow
That seemed to gild her face and show
Her full red lips and dainty nose
And her ovaline face in quiet repose.
And to her shapely body clung a wondrous
dress of emerald green,
Embedded with bouquets of golden-eyed
forget-me-nots serene.
She stood amid a whispering group, unattached,
Like Venus in her morning glory, unmatched,
Whilst all about the bustling room
Guests danced with bride and groom
To waltzing airs and ditties old
From violin, harp and trumpet rolled.
Advances stood in amorous queue,
All complimenting and hopeful too.
Elegantly she danced, a Cinderella fair,
Feather-footing thru the wax-odoured air.
I stood by balustrade and candlelight
And watched my lady's dancing flight
Until weary musicians a repose secured
And guests were to tempting dishes lured.
By swift degrees, from my twilight hide
I moved with stealth and stood by her side,
Whispering softly to her surprise
As I met the gaze of her azure eyes.
Cupid, alert, flitted to and fro, an unseen sprite
With pious mischief in his silent voice, delight
As his arrows winged fast in riotous play
And disciplined thoughts indulged in disarray.

The music restarted and we danced in
dreamy bliss,
Wanting to, but not daring to, steal a treasured kiss.
And unnoticed, and without alarm,
I led my lady with guiding word and arm
To the moonlit outer terrace where
The vibrant air was rose-perfumed and fair.
And there our love was pledged in sweet embrace,
And time stood still in that ecstatic place
Until the toll of bells came sounding clear
And echoed loudly in the bosom of my ear,
Whereupon my obedient eyes flew open wide,
And I found myself in bed alone, of love denied.
My lady fair, so beautiful a mortal to me
did seem,
Was but a figment of my wondrous dream.

ODE TO SEPTEMBER

September's rich, exotic dress
Inspires a diversity of joys,
Whose nostalgic fragrance my
memories impress
As I relive again thru childhood eyes.

And listen to the echo of an ancient song,
Winging thru the carefree scenes
That pass before my eyes along
The avenue of history that intervenes.

And where nostalgia flowers unaged
Among those happy, playful days
of youth,
Ever waiting to be paged
Among the painted leaves and autumn fruit.

That hangs invitingly from every
orchard bough
And from the wild residents of the
teeming hedgerows,
Where the rowan, crab and plum
still wander now,
Together with the hawthorn and
bramble in loudly tempting pose.

Oh, beautiful September, wherein the
spirit of autumn indulges its awe-inspiring art,
Painting by slow degrees the summer's greenery
With diverse dappled shades
that activate the joyful start
Of a colourful explosion to ignite
the changing scenery.

As deeper delve the infiltrating colours
That dance delightfully on every
beechen crown,
As the spirit of autumn thru her
unfolding tapestry wades,
Painted green and yellow with changing
hues of orange, red and brown.

Making beautiful the ageing season
That yields a multitude of joys,
Whilst fatted swallows gather with
compelling reason,
To wing away to Africa across the
bright azure skies.

Oh, let these memories forever live,
To steal, at times, with soft, nostalgic tread
Into the avenues of mind and their
pleasure again to give
When I am quietly alone or fast
asleep in bed.

AIDS

Silently it wanders –
As silently as death –
And is as coldly calculating
When it casts its net.
From partner to partner it
spreads its legions
With patient, unsuspected tread
Until, alas, too late the victim knows,
When all the guards are dead
And invasions become the
greatest threat
Without dedicated defences,
As the virus intrudes into
the nucleus of cells,
Alarming all the senses,
And panic spreads thru
the pulsating system,
Issuing warnings of disaster;
But organs are left undefended
As the virus paces faster,
Manifesting itself in diverse ways,
Generating illnesses that grow
progressively worse
And the victim's devastation
becomes irreversible,
Like the fatal conclusion of a curse.
There is no cure, alas, for Aids,
The virus with high intelligence
Hiding within the nucleus of cells
And is devoted to its diligence.
Morality is its greatest enemy,
Denying the virus its flowering spread,
But careless indulgence is the fatal knell
That lays a body low and cold and dead.

GALACTIC BLACK HOLE

Mysterious mouth of darkness
lurking in the heart of the
Milky Way galaxy,
And only identified by its
event horizon, a ring of starlight
surrounding it and stolen from
the nearest star
That is continuously spiralling
in gravitational pull round
the black hole,
That greedily devours the
energy of its victim from afar.

But why? Is the black hole an
accidental occurrence with unknown potential
Or is it an integral part of the
universal design of existence,
Implemented by the omnipotent,
creative mind of God
And regulated by the simple means of
positive and negative assistance?

Something and nothing and yet, perhaps,
the very essence of everything.
Is the black hole's definition merely
the most basic form of simplicity
When viewed thru the probing eye of
scientific thought,
And the naked truth exposed by the
illumination of its own electricity?

Into the mouth of darkness I
spiritually descended,
Faster than the speed of light
to see the recycling of matter,
Along the so-called route of the
singularity where atoms are crushed
and reduced to their rudimentary
subatomic particles
And released back into the galaxy as
undetected aspects of dark energy
in spatial scatter.

The theory of the singularity is
beyond the comprehension and
imagination of most,
Not because it's an impossibility,
but because it's a step too far
and too soon into the unknown abyss
And its significance is even a
formidable challenge to the
astrophysicist in the field,
But all is held in abeyance by
the regulated pace of evolution
under creation's omnipotent aegis.

ODE TO SPRING

Where daffodils spread their golden
trumpets far and wide
In a blazing spectacle of delight
to herald spring's arrival,
There go I with bosom friends
side by side,
To see the colourful miracle
of life's new arrival.

In nature's wild and wonderful expanse
And each petalled jewel I see I
greet with words of joy,
And I feel the presence of the
spirit of the season of romance
That caresses and nurtures all
aspects of life on Earth and
thru the vibrant air fly.

You are, oh, wondrous spring,
The spirit of existence that evokes
the renaissance of life's diversity
And its indescribable procession
of colourful and ever changing
floral beauty that the miracles bring
To the pulsating Earth's natural university.

We walk among the golden daffodils
that loudly greet
And we stop at times so that I can
admire the sea of yellow extending
along the rolling hills,
Where ewes with newborn lambs
in agile play contentedly bleat
And the living landscape my memory
with nostalgic scenes fills.

And here and there field daisies
sunbathe in clustering pose
And dandelions have already begun
to show their pregnant presence,
And, likewise too, buttercups, docks
and thistles their early identification expose,
As the spirit of spring busily
spreads its caressing presence.

And I am here, oh, wondrous spring!
In the midst of your colourful,
physical manifestation,
An ardent admirer of all the miraculous,
bountiful and beautiful facets of
life that to your presence cling,
And are nourished by the glowing
warmth of your pulsating heart
of fiery illumination.

As you develop, age and mature thru
summer to become autumn's glorious goddess,
Laden with untold fruitful jewels
on which all creatures are invited to
freely feed,
Until the appointed time when, thru
natural weariness, you are obliged
to undress
And shed your loudly painted leafy
gowns and slip quietly into winter
hibernation, from reality freed.

But for now I and faithful friends
will happily amble among your petalled
jewels, wondrous spring,
Marvelling at the immensity, diversity
and colourful complexity of your
floral beauty,
And listen to the awe-inspiring noteful
compositions that the songbirds sing.
And I understand the message
that you promote – the struggle for
survival is every form of life's
innate duty.

HAIR LOSS

Oh, little patch of glory,
I nourished you thru infancy
and youth
And loved you all thru
my growing years,
But now you fill me
with despair
And reduce me to an inner
state of tears.
Those endless hours of
gentle grooming,
With dextrous, dedicated hands,
Meticulously manipulating
Those soft and finely textured strands
Into styles of diverse fashion
That revelled in admiration
Are now, alas, with deep regret concluded
As I succumb to my humiliation.
I watched you closely thru
the years,
By slow degrees silently receding,
And oh, the ever daunting truth –
To face the world without you leading!
What dread now to enter without you
Into noisy, crowded haunts,
Believing, in a flush of shame,
To be the butt of whispered taunts.
No attentive need again for
comb or mirror,
To gently groom and style,
No ego-lifting welcome comment,
To release a self-assuring smile.
So many years bound together
And now fast approaching the final separation,

When I must stand alone, defeated.
There is no hope of reparation.
So, farewell to you, remaining strands,
Where once a multitude grew thick
and fair.
Time will heal the mental scar,
But I must confess I'll miss you, hair.

TIME AND ITS SERVANT THE CLOCK

Tick-tock, tick-tock, tick-tock –
The heartbeat of the ubiquitous clock
As it relentlessly fragments time
And is sometimes accompanied
by a musical chime
That splits the hours in quarters.
But alas, the lively interruptions
do not agree with all life's
sons and daughters,
And often lead to quarrelsome confrontation
When related to sleep deprivation,
Whereupon the chime is wisely suppressed
For the sake of peaceful rest.

But the heartbeat of the clock
continues communicating.
Thru night and day its numeralled
face and hands the hour and
minutes indicating,
Whilst the second hand above the
numerals in endless orbit sweeps,
Fragmenting the minutes and precise
time obediently keeps –
Tick-tock, tick-tock, tick-tock.

Belated gratitude to the enlightened mind
that was originally inspired to more accurately
record the passing of time.
It was a pinnacle of thought patiently
waiting for a pioneering soul to climb
And the far-sighted astronomer Galileo
seized the moment in a flash of inspiration
And mentally and physically devised the
first fragmenter of time, a pulsating tick-tock of jubilation.

The simple time fragmenter captivated
the minds of others in the scientific field,
And Galileo's innovation inspired
their thoughts to yield
Improvisations on time's theme,
Culminating in the invention of the clock and the
realisation of a dream.
And although it was hailed as the
successful harnessing of time,
With the addition of an endearing chime
Wealthy speculators used it to their
advantage and to the detriment of
marginalised employees,
Timing every aspect of their daily toil
to increase personal fortunes by degrees,
And the workforce became the time-regulated
subservient slaves to the clock,
Mentally reminded of passing time by
their innocent friend and enemy alike –
Tick-tock, tick-tock, tick-tock.

And to what end will time's
evolutionary progress lead us?
Time has our existence measured thus –
Its heartbeat is the giant fireball in space,
And its pulsating breath, the solar
wind emanating from its radiant face
That generates the energy for life's existence
Within the range of acceptable distance,
Until the energy source struggles
with its ageing distress
And increases in size to a giant in flaming dress,
Incinerating all forms of life with its
searing breath
And swallowing all its orbiting
dependants in its fiery death –
Tick-tock, tick-tock, tick-tock.

THE WARNING

Last night in bed asleep
I dreamt of Armageddon
And the devastated Earth in
the aftermath of annihilation.
"Oh, God have mercy"
came the plaintive plea
From the darkness that was day
And echoed over the seared
bones of man and beast,
In abundance strewn,
coloured blue and grey.

No songbird note,
no sound familiar,
No harmony of toil,
Only death's melancholy lament,
Winged ominously over
the poisoned soil.
And trees, those stalwart,
endearing sentinels of Earth,
In the eerie twilight lay,
Row by row in endless queue,
All dead, in direful disarray.

I saw a hobbling soul grotesque,
So vividly insane,
With tortured face in fearful pose,
A haunting mask of echoing pain.
And children cried the chilling truth
With injuries appalling,
As bodies writhed in agony,
Impatient for the final calling.

Condemned, the total diversity
of life –
The weeping Earth was dying
And extinction, the Grim Reaper,
hovering close,
Was with solemn necessity complying.
Oh, what complete and utter devastation,
Detonated by arrogant, blind
mentalities with a burning ambition
to lead.
The destruction of our beloved Earth –
I saw the suicide of greed.

FLOWER OF TRUTH

Unblemished bloom,
I found you thus,
With petals spread
and silent voice appealing,
And from your all-beguiling eye
came hauntingly
The rarest fragrance
softly stealing.

How often in youth and
after-years
I wandered far in search of you,
But never saw your bloom so fair;
and yet it was there
Wherever I roamed
in pious pose, all odour-rich,
in fullest view.
Oh, mystic flower of truth,
you were to me an undeveloped bud,
Outside the aura of tradition
And now enamoured by your scent
I dwell content and sing your song
And silent is the doubting voice
of sedition.

Bloom, bloom full,
So that I may wander thru your
petals free
And linger there to breathe the
sweetest odours
That gently ooze in endless queue,
content that I can truly see.

AUTUMN MEMORIES

When the wild west wind
sweeps over the hills
And down thru the valleys
soughing leaps,
The rain in tow in torrents spills
And surging rivers rise above
their stoutly keeps.

Whilst old autumn lies sleeping
beneath empty crowns,
Among the remnants of her
gaudy dress,
Yellows, greens, reds and browns
With nothing but aged sadness
to express.

And where winding hedgerows
stand undressed
Her fallen jewels lie in
scattered disarray,
Feasted on by denizens of the
wild in daily quest,
Over field and hill and along
rutted byways.

But oh, for the days of autumn glory
Is my nostalgic plea,
When fruitful was the mellowing story,
On orchard bough, in hedgerow and in
wood and lea.

Where sweetly plumped were the
diverse joys of autumn,
In colourful dress with loud-appealing fragrance,
The tempting apple, berry, pear
and plum,
Sensorily activating the ingredients
of divine, romantic extravagance.

And where the withering stubble
awaited the plough's attention
The foraging gleaners searched
for fallen grains,
Whilst the headland trees forlornly
stood in dormant suspension
And dark clouds from the west
announced the coming of the purging rains.

And old autumn faded into its
departing mist,
Like a pleasant dream devoured
by sleep.
Its memory is by nostalgia kissed
And all its wondrous highlights
I will in mind forever keep.

INFATUATION

Infatuation, love's empty reflection,
A spectre of joy and pain in
affairs of the heart.
It mimics love's blooming – a callous deception –
And fools the unwary into playing
a key part.

Pity the victim who is tempted
by its charm,
Embodied in beguiling smiles
and captivating eyes.
It is a thoughtless designer
of harm,
Unconcerned in its loud-appealing disguise.

The besotted spills his love
and affection
And caresses his idol with
soothing care
Until he detects the signs of rejection
And realises the object of his
desire has nothing with him
to share.

Oh, infatuation, you are an
infertile seed,
A rootless figment of the imagination,
A parasitic fantasy, a spiritual weed
Impregnated with the odour of temptation.

You hide unseen behind besotted,
inexperienced eyes,
Stoking your passionless fire,
Whilst the host a surge of short-lived
ecstasy enjoys.
And then as quickly as you manifested
yourself you unexpectedly expire.

And fade like a pleasant dream
in sleep,
When wakefulness intrudes
And sorrow spreads its mantle
and begins to weep,
And heartache activates depressing moods.

Oh, infatuation! You are a tormenting sin,
Whispering sweet nothings in the
corridors of the mind,
Knowing that you can never win.
Oh, how can you be so unkind?

THE ALCOHOLIC

The lure of the fortified drink,
A temporary escape route
from reality,
But alcohol is a demon in disguise
And a humiliating enemy of morality.

It hides away unseen in the molecules
of the fortified drink
And plies its destructive art
thru social pleasure.
And by degrees it breathes its
disarming charm,
Undoing the mental tapestry of
sobriety measure by measure.

Until the victim is overpowered
And his moral defences are shed,
As he spouts his dialogue in
incoherent slur
And unsteady is his tread.

And resented is his unpredictable mood
That sometimes erupts in violence,
And when he is forced to retreat
and finds himself all alone,
He contemplates on permanent silence.

As nearer to the great abyss he strays,
Hopelessness prominent in his
empty eyes,
And from within his confused mentality
An unknown voice silently yet
loudly cries.

It is the plea of sanity
Begging for release,
But the alcoholic drowns his
sorrow in the fortified drink
And bathes in the fumes of its
destructive peace.

And so the die is cast and
decay spreads its sorrow,
As the victim ever closer to
the brink is led
By the demon urging greater
indulgence
Until its host is thru his
own hand dead.

ABANDONED MOTHER

Alone, thru sleepless eyes I weep,
Among the dancing shadows of candlelight,
Whilst other souls untroubled sleep
Thru the quiet loneliness of night.

Here and there by little ones rest –
I can hear them softly breathe.
They are to me by nature pressed,
And I know their every vital need.

These anguished eyes must face tomorrow
Without my love, who with another fled.
Abandoned, I must hide my sorrow,
As my innocent babes must be fed.

Oh, direful humiliation, I stoop
to your lowly state
And wash away my pride with tears.
There is no creative art in hate
And I will suffer the burden of
the silent jeers.

And with resolute will and honest sweat,
These tender hands will earn the bread
To stave off the haunting threat
That fills my mind with dread.

Oh, God! I have been so blind
And only now do I begin to see,
But heaven is an elusive goal to find
And I doubt there is such a state as
worry-free.

The dwellings of those with wealth endowed
Await the labour of my hands
And my back in servility bowed,
With matted hair in sweaty strands.

Therein, alas, my future status lies,
In desperation to keep my flock.
Nobody can hear my anguished cries
And I have no valuables to hock.

But I will rise and face tomorrow –
Not because I'm inherently brave,
But for my little ones I'd beg, steal
or borrow,
For I am by nature their ever
willing slave.

STUDENTS OF INSANITY

Dens of iniquity where
the weak hide,
Unable to embrace the austere
face of reality;
Preferring instead to indulge in
idle pleasures,
They wander along the margin
of fatality.

In the foul, smoky dens
Where sorrow masquerades as joy
And porn pollutes the fragile mentalities
To win the admiration of the
wayward eye.

Drink, drugs and sex,
The idle weavers of destructive fantasy
That creates negative, stagnating dreams
All along the twilight alley.

Where the mentally blind search
for rootless excitement
And carelessly indulge in self-destruction,
Slowly suffocating in the fumes of addiction,
They stray beyond the pale of instruction.

I watched them drunkenly stagger
and stumble,
Coughing, spitting and shouting foul
Or loudly laughing in uncontrollable spasms
Whilst abusing every consonant and vowel.

And when alone in their empty hovels,
Blaming the world for their self-inflicted plight,
They indulge the useless art of self-pity
And hide away in sleep thru the night.

Then when the morn with newest
promise dawns,
They cannot face truthful reality
Without a condemning cigarette or
soul-destroying pill –
They are, alas, the eager students of insanity.

PERSONAL CONVERSATION WITH GOD

Last night in bed alone, awake,
I spoke to God
And asked Him many things:
Why was there prevalent pestilence
and horror
And why were there poor peasants
and wealthy kings?

And why manifest in the human race
Was there treachery, violence and greed?
And can a truly dedicated soul
Ever from his imprisonment be freed?

From His divine perch in the kingdom
of heaven
He wove the matter of the sun and
set it alight
And designed the Earth with its
diverse forms of life
And set it spinning to create day
and night.

Then He chose a lowly primate
And endowed it with the power
of creativity
That was, by degrees, thru evolution's
art developed
And therewith instigated man's nativity.

But man has developed into a dangerous,
volatile entity,
Perpetually tempted by power and pleasure.
He inflicts heinous crimes on his brothers
And wallows in loud and lustful leisure.

"So, oh Lord God, why do You allow
these wayward tendencies to flourish,"
I asked in telepathic language,
"When You have the power to redesign
the thoughts of man at hand
And implant in his mentality a code of
divine ethics
That would compel him to understand.

"His true role on this intriguing planet,
With all its diversely abundant resources,
From which Your plan is by
slow degrees woven
With patience, that revered quality
of unseen forces?"

"Indeed, patience is the labour
of invention," God telepathically replied
In an inspiring pulsation of thought,
And added,
"And evolution advances with slow,
careful tread
And from creation's raw materials the
changing pattern of life is wrought.

"I created Earth and all its water-dependent
forms of life,
And man was My chosen form of manifestation.
He is a volatile experiment, closely monitored,
As he struggles in his aura of mental gestation.

"Animal-based and equipped with
survival's instinctive devices,
His mentality is manipulated by an
activating, unseen germ
That stimulates an endless catalyst
of creative thought,
Perpetuated thru the secretions of
his sperm.

"And error, the perforation in
imperfect deduction,
That causes confusion and makes
every man a sinner
Is itself in truth a means of combatting stagnation
And of making man a future winner.

"Excesses and deprivations are his
self-made woes
And are instrumental in activating ills;
His vain lust for power creates imbalances
And the germination of destructive skills.

"That herald conflict and premature death,
But unaware he is the linchpin of
My plan.
He is an infant whose vain outbursts
I tolerate
As I dictate the evolutionary
progress of man.

"That will conclude with the evolutionary
fulfilment of My conception for the
spread of eternal intelligence,
Which will eventually be enacted by
the flowering of man's mental capacity.
Then I will consider his physical
suitability to exist, but without the
Stimulus for voracity!"

God silently revealed the future
to me as I lay in a trance-like state,
Digesting all that I heard in
the process.
And I wondered if what I heard
was idle fantasy
Or was it inspiration's sweet caress?

THE WIDOW

Forlorn the lady dressed in black,
In pensive mood with pale complexion
And eyes that echoed sorrow
As she mentally embraced the
thought of resurrection.

Her trembling lips obediently formed
Her sadly whispered prayers
As she nervously caressed a rosary
Beneath her greying auburn hairs.

And her teardrops flowed in rivulets,
Spilling silently on to the marble floor
And cold was the moisture
Mournfully oozing from every
lamenting pore.

"We are gathered here today,"
The preacher began his solemn address,
And the odour of incense filled
the chapel
As the widow struggled with
her distress.

"My love, like a wilted flower,
is dead
And here in this oaken coffin lies,
Forever sleeping in the lap of death,
And there too sleep my thousand joys.

"That round his living presence danced,
Like the happy notes of a
rising lark,
Echoing about the springtime sky
Until the extinguishing of the spark.

"That brightly burned with
glowing warmth
And filled my life with joy
And now, alas, that light no more
will shine
And I must the binding knot untie!"

"We pray for the soul of our
dear departed brother."
The preacher's words ate thru
the incensed air
And the mourners responded in
subdued voice
And none envied the widow's
anguished share.

The coffin bearers solemnly
slow-paced
Thru the hymn-singing procession.
It was the beginning of the last farewell –
A time to purge the conscience
thru self-confession.

"My love, forgive my angry
words of conflict
That always sprang from a
selfish need.
I would my every possession forfeit
To undo this tragic deed.

"That has stolen you away from me
Without a murmur of regret
And left me in this pit of sorrow,
Haunted by the callous face of death.

"Oh, Lord, I pray his soul is
for heaven bound,
And there for evermore with You
to dwell.
It may need to bathe in the cleansing
fields of Purgatory,
But could never descend beyond
to hell."

The cortège round the graveside gathered
And the preacher uttered the final words:
"Earth to earth, ashes to ashes, dust to dust."
And, in the nearby trees, silent
were the birds.

The coffin into its bed was lowered
And the handlers discreetly retreated,
Allowing the mourners to filter by,
And with the scattering of soil
all contact was deleted.

The widow stood in sorrowed pose
And silently whispered her last goodbyes
As she pressed a dampened handkerchief
against her weary, forlorn eyes.

"Farewell, oh love of my life.
How I dread this final parting.
Tomorrow waits, its birth a blur,
And my loneliness is but newly starting.

"No more I'll hear your happy song,
Nor kiss those lips that whispered joy.
The memories will linger ever,
But, alas, will always end with goodbye."

ODE TO A CANDLE

Oh, lowly candle spark of light,
Guide me thru the obscure night.
Cast your glow before my feet
As I pace the cobbled street.
Step by step thru blinding dark,
Every lurking danger mark.
Guide me well, oh humble light,
Brightly glowing in the moonless night,
Onward shuffling by slow degrees
Beneath the sleeping, beechen trees,
You and I together plod
By pavement, street and grassy sod.

How often I wonder how it feels
As the flame in silence steals
Down your waxen body's length,
Slowly eating all your strength,
And all for me to point the way
And take me safely to where I pray –
The hilltop church on Christmas Eve –
And there by candlelight receive
The spiritual gift of pious joy
When I call to mind the baby Boy
Who in Bethlehem one holy night
Was born in the glow of a candle's light.
And in the manger where He lay,
Asleep on a bed of golden hay,
They gathered round, man and beast,
And the lowly candle never ceased
To cast its light upon His face
And the world was told of that humble place.
Now here by oaken door I stand,
Your lighted frame in my aged hand,
And round the chapel row by row
A host of candles brightly glow.